Study to the Cultural Effectiveness of Publishing Industry

Dr. Asadollah MoazamiGoodarzi

June
2022

Title: Study to the Cultural Effectiveness of Publishing Industry
Author: Asadollah MoazamiGoodarzi
Editor: Parvaneh Khademi
Cover Designer: Aziz Mohseny
Publisher: American Academic Research, USA
ISBN: 978-1947464162

The Dedication:
Offer to My Heavenly Father
My Terrestrial Mother
My Lovely Son
And
My Spouse

Contents

Chapter 1: Introductions...9
Definitions 17
Summary.. 20

Chapter 2: Publication Industry............................ 21
Introduction.. 21
Publication Industry 22
Publication Status.. 25
The Target Group in Book Publication 27
The necessity to use universal policies and programs for... 27
Wrong policy for book distribution in Iran.............. 29
Book and Publication from the View Point of 30
What is the Result for Publication? 30
Publication Audience... 31
Publisher.. 32
Major foundations of book publication in Iran............ 32
Landmark Publishers 32
Starting point to convert book to media 33
Book Publication in Iran.. 35
Non-profitability of Publication Industry.................. 36
Speech Result.. 37
Summary.. 38

Chapter 3: Culture..41
Introduction.. 41
The Word "Culture".. 42
Culture Definition 42
Material Culture and Intellectual Culture 45
Cultural Lag 45
Utopian Culture and Real Culture............................... 46

Culture and Civilization.. 46
Cultural Values 47
Major Specifications of a Culture 48
Acculturation... 49
Unilateral Acculturation 49
Bilateral Acculturation.. 49
Sociability... 49
Cultural Norms 50
Sub Culture or Some Culture... 50
Cultural Integration 50
Cultural Aggression... 51
Counterculture... 51
Cultural Shock 51
Cultural Transformation 51
Cultural Complex 52
Public Culture (folklore).. 52
Ethnocentrism 54
Conclusion... 54
Summary.. 55

Chapter 4: Oral Culture 57
Oral Literature... 57
Specifications of Oral Literature 58
Similarities and Differences of Oral Literature for 63
Social Rituals and Oral Literature.................................. 68
Interaction of Oral Literature with Official Literature 69
Different Types of Oral Literature 71
Language.. 81
Dialectic Culture.. 83
Structuralism Approach 84
Semiology.. 85
Summary.. 88

Chapter 5: Written Culture...91
Written Literature 91
Visualization History 92

Illustrations 93
Persian Prose 94
Summary 97

Chapter 6: Past records and Consideration of the 99
History 99
Handwriting History 99
History of the Emergence of Printing in Iran 100
The Invention of Printing 102
The history of press in Iran 103
The History of Publication Industry in Iran 105
Summary 107

Chapter 7: Comparative Studies of Culture 109
Introduction 109
Culture, Views and Attitudes 111
Changing Organizational Culture 124
Culture and Strategic Management 127
Culture 127
Culture as Mental Programming 128
Culture Definition 128
Human Nature 130
Personality 132
Cultural Relativism 134
Symbols, Heroes, Rituals and Values 135
Layers of Culture 139
National Culture Differences 139

Chapter 8: Conclusion and Suggestions 147
Solutions 153

References 157

Chapter 1
Introductions

In the last years of 20th century, study of culture gradually became one of the main features of intellectual life. Probably, culture is the only concept that is used more than any other concept in social and human sciences, but it is also the vaguest concept. Deymond Williams says that is the most sophisticated words in English. Alfred Kroeber and Clyde kluckhohn, anthropologists, have proposed 200 separate definitions and usage for culture.

Culture study approaches follow French structuralism in order to understand power against culture. Cultural studies by reacting to materialistic ideologies (Specially Classic Marxism) on one hand and individualistic attitudes common in existentialism and phenomenology on the other hand, want to show that cultural structures are factors or independent forces in forming social process and human agency.

Cultural researchers believe that culture should not be considered as mere reflection of economic structures, functional needs, or personal desires, but it should be considered as a determining force in social life.

Although professors of Persian language, literature and script consider these elements as important fundamentals of Iran culture in their speeches, they do not advocate these brilliant legacies in act and do not consider them as cultural goods and do not pay attention to their roles in continuity of Iranian culture. This happens because they consider research about old literature and language, not defending fluent language, script and poem of day that is seriously threatened today, as their most important service to culture. This is so because they do not accurately know what is culture and cultural continuity; they also do not know that old language, literature and script are only a small part of our language and literature. They are not aware of relation between culture and language and literature and do not know that in case of rupture in this relationship, decline and rupture in culture and literature occurs. Since they have not understood importance of this issue, they do not try to establish these connections or do not find solutions to prevent these weaknesses and ruptures in these vital connections.

Culture is considered as one of pillars of development in any country. Culture is a complex mix of knowledge, sciences, arts, regulations and laws, traditions and shortly, it is all habits and taught that a human as a member of society acquires them; this person has duties and obligations entrusted to the community.[1] Zoveidi says: Culture includes all the habits of a society, or if society is considered as an organized collection of people that have certain lifestyle, culture means this same lifestyle.[2] According to the concepts of culture and all above mentioned, the culture and cultural elements are learned not innate and in addition culture and its elements are

---

1. SeyyedJavdein (2004), 611
2. Zoveidi (2000), 6

intended to satisfy the needs and requirements of people. Also culture and its elements should be appropriately provided to the public and people who need it; so they should be returned to cultural goods and services so that people can readily use them. Given this content, cultural services and goods can be defined as: "a useful and applicable object or service that is produced by some people in the society to meet the cultural needs of others".[1]

Any society has a special pattern of "cultural generalities" for its own that includes essential human organizations such as social organization, religion, political structure, economic organization and financial culture (tools, weapons, Clothes). But glossaries are also sometimes called culture because such books and their content are representative of common culture of a nation with common language and specific culture of scientific tradition of some researchers in human societies. Since production requires some tools to provide the best bed for it, publication industry is one of the most important one of those tools that should be studied more and more accurately.

Publishing means making public or conveying information to people, especially through press. Press is an area in which all practioners of graphic and related subjects generate base of production and reproduction of a magazine, newspaper, or book in cooperation with each other.[2] Publication industry covers a wide range of press, publication and distribution in different ways. Through centuries, book publication has been an innovative industry and in some times, it has been the main business in some countries.[3]

1. Royaie & Rashidpour (2008), 20-21
2. Mesghali (2011), 2-3
3. Semsar ,Mohammad (2012), 53

Culture is a collection of values, beliefs, understanding and deduction, and thinking methods that members of an organization have common interfaces in them and this is what is thought to newcomers as a correct phenomenon.

Culture represents the unwritten and invisible part of human identity that obligates one to incredible beliefs and values.

Traditional values lead to more strength and stability of organization and as a result of them newcomers understand causes of activities and events.[1]

Cultural Identity: Cultural identity is dominant on all identities and has interrelationship with them. Average of individual identities in collective scale, in addition to education, sociability and traditions of these individuals, make cultural identity that is represented in different individual, political and social contexts.[2]

Lambert and Gardner (1982) studied foreign language learners in Canada, America and Philippines to identify role of attitude and incentive in language learning. They divided a set of attitudes to two main types of incentive namely instrumental and synthetic according their studies. Instrumental incentive reflects practical and specific purposes of learning a language, for example job development, studying in foreign countries, passing an important test. Synthetic incentive occurs when a learner wants to merge himself with cultural group of the second language and become part of it. Lambert found that synthetic incentive has high correlation with high score in language proficiency test. The result is that the purpose of high level of synthetic incentive is to be more successful than instrumental incentive in learning the second

---

1. Stanley Dayris (2007)
2. Alikhani(2009), *2007 Quoted from Hosseini Anjadani*

language, although there may be some exceptions. Shortly after these findings, other scientists reported conflicting findings. Lukmany (1982) studied learning English in Indian students whose first language was Marathi and concluded that those who had more instrumental incentives, got higher scores in English language proficiency tests.

According to Bloom and Campers (1972) people constantly make their identities using each of languages they have learned fluently. Lambert and Garner (1982) by studying foreign language learners in Canada, America and Philippines concluded that in the process of foreign language learning, learner tries to merge himself in the cultural group of the second language and become part of it. In contrast, Norton (2000) showed interrelationship between foreign language and identity of language learners. On one hand, learner identity has effects on learning foreign language and on the other hand, investing on one language results in learning a wide range of symbolic and material resources and promotion of cultural capital and identity of individuals.

According Bordew and Pearson, cultural capital refers to the knowledge and mindsets that describe different groups and categories in relation with specified sets of social forms.[1] Norton used the word investment to describe ambiguous incentives and desires that language learners may have for the target language. If language learners invest on the second language, they will do the same to understand and recognize it. This recognition shows that they will cover a wide range of symbolic and material resources and value of their cultural capital will increase.

In a research titled "Language and Identity" it is noted that in recent years, thinkers and experts of human and

---

1. Norton (2000), 10

social sciences have paid attention to language as core of culture and key element in forming identity. In this regard, emphasis has been on role of foreign language in forming identity. On this basis, different theoretical approaches such as viewpoints of Vorf and Sapier, Soosoor, Berger, Lukman, Bakhtin and others have put emphasis on the role of language in identity.Considering this, the purpose of this paper is studying connection and relationship between learning foreign language and identity of individuals of statistical population in individual, social, national and cultural dimensions. This study is a social survey and research data are gathered by questionnaire. Statistical population includes students of foreign language faculties and institutes of Kashan in 2012; of this population 180 students were selected randomly as research sample and were studied. Results of this research show a positive relationship between fluency in foreign language and individual identity (r = 237.0) and its negative relationship with national identity (r = 173.0) on certainty level of 99 and 95 percent. Also, positive correlation between being interested in foreign language and measure of social and cultural identity that are respectively r = 147.0 and r = 200.0 was verified on certainty level of 99 percent.[1]

It was Cheng that in 1994 analyzed cultural values represented in Chinese magazines in from 1982 to 1992. His research showed that "modernity", "technology" and "quality" were dominant values through these years.[2] Since this research aims addressing those values that are of symbolic value and can represent some problems of culture of the country, so some of values suggested by Cheng

---

1. Niazi & others (2012)
2. Chan & Cheng (2002), 5

(1994) were analyzed including tradition, modernity, plurality, individualism, youth, family, showing respect to old people and nationalism.

Increasing acceleration of changes in history of communication world on one hand, and insufficient growth of publication industry as the main transmitter of knowledge and information and the industry having the most influence on culture on the other hand, is a problem that should be addressed seriously. However, publishing industry is a new industry in developing countries and if print and printing were not established in Iran, book and press would never be created in modern meaning. Book publication is one of the main indicators of intellectual and moral emission and the most important intellectual and cultural evolution and criteria of development, but in our country, publication industry and its effects on society is an important area that has not been explored because of unknown reasons.

One of its effects can be effects on culture. Since according to Klaken "culture is a part of environment that is created by man".[1] In this research we want to study situation of publication industry in Iran and then study its effects on culture.

Since researchers obviously know that publication certainly has effects on culture and there is no doubt about this effect, researcher divides culture into two parts: oral and written. In doing so, researcher wants to study measure of effect of publication industry on any part of culture and compare them. With this comparison, not only amount of

---

1. Vosoughi, Mansoor & Aliakbar NickKholgh (1999), 151-152

effect is measured, but it will be decided that which part of culture is more affected and finally some solutions to improve it and its effectiveness will be proposed.

Publication industry has been one of the most useful and biggest inventions of human and a tool for transferring thoughts and emotions of many scientists throughout history. This industry made education and research that were once in monopoly of a certain group, possible and available for common people. Also, this industry has preserved results of high intellectual and scientific thoughts of scientists.

Role of publication industry, as role of hygiene, in human life and his cultural needs, has been of critical effect on improvement of life quality and scientific developments. Results of positive effects of publication, direct or indirect, are obvious in all aspects of human life. This industry is such interconnected with human being and is of such importance in his cultural growth that he cannot be isolated from it; wherever he goes and whatever he does is related to this industry.

Before addressing to topic of culture, we should know that cultural values form the main core of culture. Such definition is obvious in a viewpoint that its basis is culture: culture can be considered as a collection of values, ideas, norms, and artifacts and other meaningful symbols that help people to make relationships, interpret relations and evaluate others as members of society. Culture is a collection of learnable values and behaviors that is transferred from a generation to next generation and makes every society unique in this regard.[1]

As it was noted, cultural values make central part of culture of any country; but it should be noted that value

---

1. Gidenz (1387), 55-56

has many definitions and different people have different ideas about it. The definition that is presented here, explains what cultural values mean for us. Cultural values are "dominant ideas and rules guiding thought and act" in a society and also a powerful force to form incentives, lifestyles, and product selection by consumers.[1] But this point should be considered that capacity and intensity of cultural values are different from one culture to other culture. Capacity refers to this point that if a cultural value is considered positive or negative. Intensity represents strength or importance of a value in a culture. For example, in some American cultures, value of showing respect to elders has negative capacity and mean intensity. Many Americans instead of oldness, value youth. But in countries such as Korea, Japan and Mexico, respect to elders has positive capacity and very high intensity.[2] By definitions of culture and considering that culture has influenced all aspects of our life, factors and tools such as publication industry affect it.

Definitions

Publication Industry: Publication industry covers a wide range of publication, press and distribution affairs. Book publication has been an innovative industry for centuries and it has been considered as the main business of countries for some times.[3]

Publishing: Publishing means making public or conveying information to people, especially through press. Press is an area in which all practioners of graphic

---

1. Tese & et. al (1989)
2. Chan & Cheng (2002), 388
3. Semsar, Mohammad (2012), 53

and related subjects generate base of production and reproduction of a magazine, newspaper, or book in cooperation with each other.[1]

Culture: Farhang is composed of two parts: "far" that is a prefix and in Avesta and Achaemenian Persian is referred as (FRA) that means "ahead", and "hang" that has Avestan root and means "sang" and includes "A" as prefix that means will and intent; it has been "farhang" in Pahlavi language.

Farhang (culture) has different meanings in dictionaries including a branch that is laid on earth and when it buds in other spot of earth, it is planted in soil of other spot, ganat mouth, a place that water comes out of it and high rise of qanat water.

- Farhang has other meanings including opinion, contraption and soberness.

- Farhanj that is homophone with Shatranj (chess) means knowledge and wisdom and curtsy.

- Farhangidan and farhanjidan (making cultural) means traditions and pedagogy.

- Farhanjideh or farhangideh (civilized) means one who is or can be nurtured.

- Farhanjeh means courteous, affable, good hearted and beautiful people.

Culture in Latin means to plant, improve and making fertile;[2] in other words, it includes all intellectual and material achievements of human being throughout history that is transferred from one generation to the next generation.[3] Everything, material or non-material, that is

---

1. Mesghali (2011), 2-3
2. Vosoughi & NickKholgh (1999), 149
3. Rabani & Shahnooshi (2001), 37

created by human being in life phases, is covered by concept of culture.[1]

Material Culture: A collection of phenomena that is tangible and measureable by scientific and quantitative measures is referred to as material culture; these phenomena include industry and instrumentation, making clothes, weaving and many other things.

Intellectual or non-material Culture: This culture includes subjects that are qualitative, are not measureable by quantitative measures and cannot be evaluated and compared easily, such as traditions, beliefs, language, handwriting, art and ... .[2]

Information Technology: a set of tools that can be used to transform data into information and transfer it to different places in different distances. Computer and telecommunication networks are physical tools that are known as "information technology" and the network that information technology appears in it is called internet. Nowadays internet is so developed that has connected millions of computers and hundreds millions of computers throughout the world.[3]

Information: Information means any news, image, and event and ... that is a reflection of fact.[4] Data that are processed such that is meaningful for recipient and has subjective or real value in current or future-related decisions is referred to as information. Relation of data

---

1. Mac Klank, et. al (1993), 173
2. GharaieMoghaddam (1995), 149
3. Kahen (1995)
4. MohseniyanRad (1992), 367

and information is similar to relation of raw material and final product; in other words, information processing system processes data and converts them to information.[1]

Summary

In 20th century, study of culture is one of the main features of mind and intellectual life of human being and probably is the one concept that is applicable in human and social sciences; meanwhile, it has vaguest concept because up to now no comprehensive definition of it has been proposed that all scientists accept it.

Many factors affect culture. One of these factors is publication industry. Publication industry covers a wide range of publishing, press and distribution affairs in different ways. Increasing acceleration of changes in history of communication world on one hand, and insufficient growth of publication industry as the main transmitter of knowledge and information and the industry having the most influence on culture on the other hand, is a problem that should be addressed seriously. This paper studies current situation of publication industry and explores its effects on culture (material or intellectual culture).

In order to achieve to these purposes and to find solutions, this research seeks to answer this question that how is current situation of publication industry in Iran. Also, this paper studies effects of publication industry of Iran on culture (oral and written) and besides comparing these effects to determine which kind of culture is more affected, some solutions are proposed to improve situation of publication industry in Iran.

---

1. Ahanchi (2007), 264

Introduction

If we look through a far past to publication industry we will witness for the slow and gradual process of publication industry after Gutenberg and the industrial revolution after 17th century paved the way for its great developments. In 18th century, publication industry continued its slow development and we observed its remarkable effect on development and innovation in publication. In its general meaning, publication defines with changing thoughts, believes and emotions of a person or a group of people to a written and recorded work and to publish it for other people usage. Book publication has been an important and influencing indicator over culture, it is now, and it always attracted the attention of high-class officials and researchers. However, with regard to the importance of press and publications in political and social life of a country and specially its elegant role and simultaneously its profound effect in cultural development, it reminds us the important mission of every person. The role of every human being in order to bring about the suitable ground to perform the great mission of printing, publication and press for the promotion and growth of a country.

Publication Industry

Publication industry covers an expanded range of printing, publication, and distribution in different methods. Book publication has been a creative industry during centuries and it has been the major job for most countries.[1]

Publication and press encompasses different types such as magazines, newspapers and books and internet sites for the recent years. Publication of the information series, in fact, has been in text, picture or both of them, which will duplicate.

Publication is equal to the word, public informing or to make it public, especially by the help of printing and publication. Press is a ground in which all graphic specialists and its related courses help each other to pave the way to produce and duplicate a magazine, newspaper or a readable and attractive book.[2]

Book is the common and old way of providing information, which delivers with different subjects. Here commercial, educational and professional ones are among the pioneer ones as university and educational books shape half of the publication market.

Unfortunately, here we face with some wrong point of views about audience need in publication industry; some publishers whose only goal is to produce and publish fixed amount of book in any feasible way and without paying attention to audience need. It might be that they do not concern about quality and content type and they do not

1. Semsar, Mohammad (2012), 53
2. Mesqali (2011), 2-3

think about the decreasing process of audience taste toward books. The existence of some rival Medias (television, internet and radio) is influencing too.

In a general conclusion, we mention to the main concerns of publication industry in Iran as follows:

1. The necessity of holding a long-term programming and strategy for working. Publishers' goals can be economic and financial or cultural; both of these goals can work together simultaneously.

2. Demand anticipation. Even if we have a correct, modern strategic programming, it might be that this anticipation includes some axiomatic errors. Its abstract cause reflects in the type of product of publishers.

3. Knowledge of discussion management. Publication organization in Iran works traditionally and individually.

4. Organization of discussion cultural. For private publication, owner generally has the role of complex manager too.

5. Pay attention to the need and taste, making need and taste for audience.

6. Enjoying from industrial or traditional publication and governmental or non-governmental one.

7. Pay attention to the providing chain of publication industry. It's includes production and provision of content.[1]

For publication industry either in private or governmental section, we feel the intense need for a political thought among the related custodians and human force. Nowadays we encounter with huge amount of complaints by publishers in Medias (newspaper and television) and even in cyber space about the increase of

---

1. Tahmasebi, et. al (2012), 7 -15

paper price, absence of study culture and decrease of productions.[1] Publication concept from printing invention up to now faced many changes. If publication concept was printing and book duplication, pamphlet or other similar cases, today it relates in other informing resources including tape, different movies, video tapes, diskette, and optical compact disks. As general, there is one concept forever and that is publication which exists as a loop between (author, translator, editor and ...) and publisher. As general (one author or a group of authors, translator, editor or one organization) bring about works. Then they deliver it to the publisher and he print it through some processes, distributes it and finally gives it the it's related user.

Publication is one of the important and valuable cultural actions, which produces in every community and culture in accordance with its fundamental ideal infrastructures and it goes inside the all classes of community and leads in the promotion of several cultural, economic, - social views. Publication holds a special defined view and showcase. This view in fact manifests manners of people of thought, culture, and writing. Whereupon, thinking about this showcase leads us to the views of cultural efforts of dependents to one culture and language. Most of professionals define publication as one of the thought making and culture-developing field. They believe that culture and identity of every country depends on roots for written culture of that society. In another way, the originality of written culture from public thought and culture demands a process made, and revolutionized by the culture-makers of that community. Iran also

---

1. *Op. cit*

through enjoying from its own civilizational capabilities during history used this thought developing facility and tried to preserve its culture in different periods. There is no doubt that today written culture of Iran continued from the first civilization days up to now is among one of the most fruitful cultures in the world. Today we see poems of Saadi Shirazi over the door of united nation organization or in the world museum we face with Iranian written culture such as Hafez, Molana, Khayyam, Ferdowsi, Attar Neishabouri and ..., these are all witnesses for the related culture- Makers efforts. In another way, these culture-makers sent the sound of one culture to the smart ears of other worlds during different historical periods and on the other hand tried to preserve and guarantee the survival of their depth culture. There is no doubt that today; the written culture of Iran covers an expanded display of these efforts. In case that we are going to continue the subject of preserving Persian written culture through a glance over publication record for those Iranian people who live in foreign countries , there is no doubt that the role and influence of authors and other related people to create a written culture holds a valuable, lofty place.[1]

Publication Status

Publishers: the number of publishers currently is more than 5000, this number in comparison with the first half of 70 decade had remarkable growth, but the main point in not the number of publication license, but the important point is the number of active and productive publishers. Year 2001 has been a year for newly come

---

1. Tondro Saleh (2005)

Book and Publication from the View Point of National and Public Interests

Book is a financial and cultural wealth, which in national scope and cultural side and society level and for all readers is a wealth and labor force and scientific and cultural movement. It is an economic production and the more important of them it is a picture of thought and emotions border, which shows the historical and cultural identity of a nation or it, provides country's culture to the other countries. Every book includes the first message coming from author mind to the readers mind. Book production and usage are two main bases for the publication life cycle. Three components are remarkable in book cycle: 1) Creation; 2) production; 3) Recreation.

Creation is a complex process, which providing facilities for it need expanded and long term, harmonized policies and in publication production section, the most important action is to bring facilities for production, removing obstacles, and decrease of production expenses. Reproduction is a higher level than publication production, action, and reaction for the produced and delivered book to society demands all time, effort and wealth from the starting point to the last step of book publication, so it shall come to its end.

What is the Result for Publication?

Publication is an industry to produce a cultural good called book. Book publication is like an art of sending message. A message received from publication throws to other point through knowledge and technic, capital, skill and other abilities from one point to other point. If this throwing comes to the right goal, it can be effective. This action is watchable even in radio and television programs, if a program is successful to meet different listeners and viewers' criterions correctly, it will be successful. Publishers shall pay attention to this point that book publication is not just a printing duplication; publication is a series of values comes from the produced book. If publication can select the right way from its starting point, it will not go to the wrong line. Publication is the technic and art of duplication and production of readable, watchable, and hearable materials. Publication is a need - oriented action by its entity or it is an audience-oriented activity. A successful publisher can develop his book market and to attract a plenty of audiences. In book publication, audience is all people having common specifications and these specifications influence on the published book.

Publication Audience

One of the effective elements in publication is buyer-reader, which can shape book market economy because he helps the publisher through buying books whereupon, publisher can receive his expenses. General people and ordinary readers are the most complex issues for recognizing audiences all over the world. Recognizing their interests and taste is not easy. Never and in no conditions and in no community, we cannot suppose publication audience as one or to consider them in one area. Even one type of audiences has different categorizations and types. If publisher asks himself that to whom I am publishing, and if he enjoys from a precise and clear-cut picture of his audience, he comes to the main step. An audience-oriented and demand-oriented publication is a targeted publication.

police system that had many negative effects on book publication. That was a healthy period for thoughts and book publication. Years 1951 and 1952 was a meeting period for nationalizing oil industry. These political events had many influence on publications. After nationalizing the oil industry, prime ministry period of Doctor Mohammad Mosadeq and his campaigns and Ayatollah Kashani together with his followers shaped with fighting against strangers. On year 1952, curfew established in Iran and some newspapers like Bakhtare Emrooz by management of Doctor Hossein Fatemi performed liberality activities. Publication actions executed after Islamic Revolution brought about positive revolutions. Some of them over structure and some of them infrastructure, but our publication industry demands more infrastructural actions.

Non-profitability of Publication Industry

Non-profitability of publication industry in Iran has cultural reasons because in Iran, book is a decorative and fantasy device. Until book becomes as one of the life necessities and problems solving, its purchase will not be necessary. If people learn to solve their problems through referring to books, for example to repair a device or access to address or training their child, book will enter to family purchasing program like many other life necessities. Book and book reading in our country in fact is for acquiring cultural and scientific privileges not for solving routine life problems. On the other hand, book reading is a holy affair in our country, although holiness is desirable but this holiness is an obstacle for entrance of book reading among different people of society (literate, illiterate, workers, farmers, housewives), among all institutions (hospitals, jails, kindergartens, elderly care centers, entertainment centers,

throwing comes to the right goal, it can be effective. This action is watchable even in radio and television programs, if a program is successful to meet different listeners and viewers' criterions correctly, it will be successful. Publishers shall pay attention to this point that book publication is not just a printing duplication; publication is a series of values comes from the produced book. If publication can select the right way from its starting point, it will not go to the wrong line. Publication is the technic and art of duplication and production of readable, watchable, and hearable materials. Publication is a need - oriented action by its entity or it is an audience-oriented activity. A successful publisher can develop his book market and to attract a plenty of audiences. In book publication, audience is all people having common specifications and these specifications influence on the published book.

Publication Audience

One of the effective elements in publication is buyer-reader, which can shape book market economy because he helps the publisher through buying books whereupon, publisher can receive his expenses. General people and ordinary readers are the most complex issues for recognizing audiences all over the world. Recognizing their interests and taste is not easy. Never and in no conditions and in no community, we cannot suppose publication audience as one or to consider them in one area. Even one type of audiences has different categorizations and types. If publisher asks himself that to whom I am publishing, and if he enjoys from a precise and clear-cut picture of his audience, he comes to the main step. An audience-oriented and demand-oriented publication is a targeted publication.

Publisher

In accordance with their publication foundation validity or any other principle, which shapes their publication, publishers categorize in two parts:

1. One foundation publishers
2. Multi foundations publishers

One foundation publishers receive a ready work in one version, and they duplicate it in hundreds or thousands versions through their capital, specialty, and skills, they leave them in distribution network and finalize their job. One foundation publisher and publication has a repetitive point of view. Multi-foundation publishers are closer to the publication goals, which are three elements of relation, interaction, and influence; they relate elements with each other. Multi-foundation viewpoint does not restrict to duplication, he pays attention to attitude, scope, and productive activity. Work creative and work selective publication as the two different approaches toward publication and like two realities stay with each other. Until there are activism and action decision, we have these two elements together.

Major foundations of book publication in Iran

Amirkabir, Jafari, for a 25 years period of activity, was the major foundation for book publication in Iran. This situation acquired through its founder specifications and it is possible to find it's similar among all landmark publication managers without exception.

Landmark Publishers

A few amount of publisher enjoy from the title of "landmark" They are work makers, need makers, pioneer, retrospective publishers. They attract minds toward novel

and new thoughts, new works, viewpoints, different attitudes and analysis, close areas and lines, new plans and novel approaches, for that reason they bring about new adventures and they are even makers. They influence on researches, educations, searches and cultural activities.

Starting point to convert book to media

Book publication in Iran, is the starting point to convert book to a public Media up to now and based on book production indexes, it passed from different major steps and a plenty of side steps. Here we mention to the major steps:

1. Publication before printing (from invention and usage of script in Iran until printing entrance).

2. It is since the entrance of printing technology, and duplication publication; until start of intellectual, political movements, constitutionalism, and anti-authoritarian thoughts.

3. It is since the establishment of the constitutionalism system until political area in 1931 and establishment of new institutions influencing on publication and its related jobs.

4. since 1931 to new social- political period established after 1941, August (about the time of Iran occupation

5. From first of 1941 decade until military cope

6. from 1953 until 1962

7. from 1963 until 1971

8. From 1972 until exploding publication of forbidden works from second half of 1978.

9. From Islamic Revolution and start of 1979 up to now which is a quarter of a century and it divides to some subsidiary areas.

1-9 Suspension and uncertainty period

2-9 Transfer period

3-9 Remarkable but short growth period

4-9 Depression Period (this period is between 1979 until 1991

5-9 from1992 until 1998

6-9 from 1999 until 2003

7-9 from 2004 onwards

For these categorizations, every period has general and common specifications, which separate it from other periods. Active publishers of country (active, based on this definition that he has not published less than 24 books annually that is less than 2 books monthly), in accordance with their starting point for their job, they passed different publication areas, whereupon inevitably they took effect from each period requirements. Amirkabir established by Jafari is not an exception here and it is possible to determine its location precisely through more descriptive investigation of periods. Abdolrahim Jafari established Amirkabir on 1949, in 12 years of publication after 1941, August. This publication period enjoys from some specifications:

1. It has relative freedom

2. It takes effect from political atmosphere

3. It has more tendency toward left party

4. It has a very weak economic motivation because of bad economy condition of country

5. There is a clash between traditional and modern tendencies but none of them conquered completely.

6. According to these cases, book production is the most important cultural production in country.

Book Publication in Iran

Since long time ago, prescribers, calligraphers, booksellers, gilders, cover makers, binders and people like them, have been active in book publication job, however book publication background with printing device, since its first entrance to Iran started on 1369 [AD]. For a special period, Armenian had the monopoly for using printing devices in different parts of Iran like Esfahan, Ourmie, and south of Iran and they published holy works of Christians. Revolutions in publication in Qajarie period are as follows:

1. Publication of several books in crown prince period for Abbas Mirza

2. Publication of the firs newspapers for country and enhancement of these newspapers until the constitutionalism area

3. Establishing Darolfonoon and publishing scientific and educational books.

During first Pahlavi area (from 1925-1961) Iran entered in a new cultural and political period. There was a great tendency toward industrialization like developed countries such as Germany in this period. However, the cultural and economic infrastructures for this tendency did not exist and it was against with public culture. Imperative education was a great cultural revolution in this period, which made many families to register their children in elementary schools, for that reason, schools established instead of Maktabkhane. The general literacy had approximate development in this period, they compiled new educational books, and they established printing offices and private and governmental institutions. One of the specifications of this period was an autocratic-

police system that had many negative effects on book publication. That was a healthy period for thoughts and book publication. Years 1951 and 1952 was a meeting period for nationalizing oil industry. These political events had many influence on publications. After nationalizing the oil industry, prime ministry period of Doctor Mohammad Mosadeq and his campaigns and Ayatollah Kashani together with his followers shaped with fighting against strangers. On year 1952, curfew established in Iran and some newspapers like Bakhtare Emrooz by management of Doctor Hossein Fatemi performed liberality activities. Publication actions executed after Islamic Revolution brought about positive revolutions. Some of them over structure and some of them infrastructure, but our publication industry demands more infrastructural actions.

Non-profitability of Publication Industry
Non-profitability of publication industry in Iran has cultural reasons because in Iran, book is a decorative and fantasy device. Until book becomes as one of the life necessities and problems solving, its purchase will not be necessary. If people learn to solve their problems through referring to books, for example to repair a device or access to address or training their child, book will enter to family purchasing program like many other life necessities. Book and book reading in our country in fact is for acquiring cultural and scientific privileges not for solving routine life problems. On the other hand, book reading is a holy affair in our country, although holiness is desirable but this holiness is an obstacle for entrance of book reading among different people of society (literate, illiterate, workers, farmers, housewives), among all institutions (hospitals, jails, kindergartens, elderly care centers, entertainment centers,

sport centers). We shall know that government role to distribute studying and book-reading culture does not restrict to the distribution of book discount paper, holding fairs, however government shall organize and manage studying, and book reading culture through a long term planned programming for modification of education, economy and culture structure and by a national movement. Government shall modify rules, regulations and by-laws and to let unions to grow and to help them to take action for solving publication problem especially marketing and distribution.

Speech Result

Findings talks about the great influence of book in civilized countries. Our civilization is what we call it "book culture". Books influence us through thousands methods, book publication history is also technology invention history which combines with society changes with regard to technology invention and development of people knowledge. Three important inventions, which paved the way for book publication is handwriting, paper and printing. Human thoughts publication is as old as human history and human always tried to share his knowledge with others, in this regard, the invention of printing in 15th century was a milestone in sharing thoughts and ideas of people. Today book publication is one of the greatest cultural and economic activities of human being. Book publication in Iran is the most important cultural industry or it is the most important and the major cultural element. Publication facilitates accessibility to information channels and it is a communicational and connecting bridge between generations, communities, cultures, and civilizations, between life and illumination history. Without publication history, it is not possible to write about illumination and most of the cultural efforts. Here press is one of the most popular and the most outstanding products of industrial society. In this world, using newspaper and magazine, is an obvious criterion for measuring the amount of progress and development of every country. It is an industrial production and item and it is a mental creation, which surely mentions to the valuable role and influence of authors and others for creation of a written cultures.

Summary

This chapter mentions to the investigation of publication industry condition and its main concerns. In knowledge area, information is a power. Today people and organizations, which understand the real value of information (compiled knowledge) and their own knowledge, are more successful, but activity in knowledge situation is not a simple job. Information management system works with information. Publication is the most important and the major cultural industry and it is the major cultural element of each country. In its public meaning, publication is changing thoughts, believes and emotions of a person or group of people to a written and recorded work and to publish it for the usage of other people. Book publication has been and it is an important, influencing, and index in culture and it always attracted the attention of officials and researchers. However, with regard to the importance of press and publications in political and social life of a country and especially with regard to the elegant and depth role of publication in cultural development, it reminds us the important mission of every person. It is a mission to facilitate the implementation of a great mission of printing, publication, and press for the promotion and development of a country. Most experts define publication as one of the thought making, culture distribution grounds and they believe that culture, and identity of each country depends on the roots that society takes from its written culture. In other way, the originality of written culture in public culture and thought for every community demands a process made, processed and revolutionized by culture maker of that society. The wrong policy for the distribution of book and cultural packages is the most important problem of printing industry. In this chapter, we talked about publication industry, publisher (producer), audience (user) and book and publication history.

Introduction

Nowadays people use the word "culture" with its different meanings and they use it too much as a new fashion idiom but no one knows it's right meaning.

Today everybody talks about culture, but no one knows its correct and precise meaning. For that reason, we feel the absence of a written text and a precise research about "culture" in our country. Ethnography is one of the important courses of sociology, it shall be one of its lessons, and it shall have precise definition and division to prevent it from having different and paradox descriptions. In past years "culture" defined as training and polite and polite used as synonym for "culture"; but today it takes another meaning and it mentions to the "foreign meaning" for culture. Even those culture lovers unfortunately do not know the precise and correct meaning of its sociology, public uses it frequently without having clear concept of it in their mind, where upon, it is necessary to provide you with a scientific and precise definition and description before starting the main discussion.

Among thousands of different meaning for "culture," researcher chose some examples.

The Word "Culture"

The word "Culture" shapes with two parts, "far" as prefix and in Archimedean Persian and in Avesta , used as (FRA) and " Hang" comes from Sang Avesta root meaning "pulling" and with prefix "A" meaning intention and it has been "Farahang" in Pahlavi language.

"Culture" in different meaning like "vocabulary book", a branch of plants putting inside the ground and it come out in other place and they grows in another place, aqueduct span, gulley's span where water comes out, idiomatically when aqueduct shows itself.

- Culture has another meaning: Idea, wisdom and thinking
- Farhanj homophone with Shatranj means science, knowledge, wisdom and polite.
- Farhangidan and Farhanjidan mean customs and training.
- Farhanjide or Farhangide means someone who accepts training or someone who is a trained person.
- Farhanje means polite, beaming, and good character and good face people.
- Culture in its Latina root means cultivation, development, land cultivation, and fertility.[1]

Culture Definition

- Edward Barent Taylor: "Culture is a complex series encompassing knowledge, believes, arts, ethics, rules, habits and any other capability that human being acquires as a member of community".

---

1. Vosooqi, Mansoor & NikKholgh, AliAkbar (1999), 149

- Visler: "it is a complex series of activities learned by human being group."
- Malinovsky: "Culture is simply a generality of a cloth having usable devices and items, it is the major specification for different group, imaginations, jobs, believes and human customs."
- Bos: "Culture includes those actions common among a group of people and it transfers from one generation to the other one and from one society to the other community."
- Ralf Linten: "Culture is a combination of school manner which transfers from one generation to the other one by special members of a society and it is common among people."
- Herskuits: "Culture is a life method for a group of people, society shapes with people and their methods and culture."
- Yank: "Culture is faces for normal and common actions in a socialized group or in a community and it shapes with financial and non-financial factors."
- Vili: "Culture is a system of habitual paradigms and answering which are coherent."
- Agbern & Nimkef: "Culture includes intellectual and material specifications organized to provide major needs for human being."
- Kelaken: "Culture is a part of environment created by human being."[1]
- Sarter: "Culture comes from human being; in case of researching, it is the only mirror which can show its face to human being."[1]

---

1. Vosooqi, Mansoor & Nikkholgh, AliAkbar (1999), 151-152

- The real and visible result of human efforts in social life generally called "Culture".
- Herskuits: "Culture is a part of environment made by human being and took influence from him."
- Culture is a series of structures, postures, ideas, and values of a society, which transfers from one generation to the other one.
- Culture means literature, sciences, and beautiful arts.
- Every social action is Culture.
- Culture means knowing the generalities for social realities and selection of different scenarios in community for crisis controlling.[2]
- Culture is the manner and believes specification acquired by special community members.[3]
- Culture is synonym with ethics and cultural life means ethical life.
- Culture mentions to all material and intellectual achievements of human being during his history, which continuously transfers from one generation to the other one.[4]
- Everything material or non-material made during life of human being come under the concept of culture.[5]
- Culture means specific life method of each group or it is all products, savings, customs, rule, believes, arts and public knowledge transferred from one generation to the other one.[6]

---

1. Rabbani, Rasool & Shahnooshi, Mojtaba (2001), 33
2. *Ibid*, 34
3. Bros Koen (1993), 37
4. Rabbani, Rasool & Shahnooshi, Mojtaba (2001), 37
5. Alfred Mac Kelankli, et. al (1993), 173
6. GharaeeMoqadam, Amanollah (1995), 148

Material Culture and Intellectual Culture

Culture encompasses two main parts: material and intellectual culture.

- Material culture is a series of phenomenon, which are tangible and measurable through scientific and quantity criterions like industry and instrumentation, cloth preparing, home construction, weaving and many other things.

- Non-material or intellectual culture includes those subjects with quality aspect, which is not measurable through quantity measuring, and their comparison and evaluation is not easy. Like customs, believes, literature, language, handwriting, art, etc.[1]

- Material culture includes a part of cultural elements that are palpable, measurable, assessable and compareable.

- Non - material or intellectual culture includes those subjects with quality aspect, you cannot make comparison for them, and they are not measurable.[2]

Cultural Lag

- It is chronological span between change in material culture and its related changes in non-material culture.[3]

- Cultural delay or cultural lag means lag or awkwardness in implementation and intellectual culture elements from material culture, which exists proportionately in all communities.[4]

---

1. Qaraee Moqadam, Amanollah (1995), 149
2. Vosooqi, Mansoor & Nikkholgh, Aliakbar (1999), 162
3. Bros Koen (1995), 59
4. Qaraee Moqadam, Amanollah (1995), 162

Utopian Culture and Real Culture

-    Some actions forbidden intensely but we observe them in privacy. The utopian culture is what people really do.[1]

Culture and Civilization

- Civilization means a series of believers and customs acquired through industrial arts, beautiful arts, science and religion and it is synonym with culture.[2]

- B. Adamz: "it is a complex governmental institution of civilization."

- Arnold Twin B.: "It is religious and moral civilization."

- Alfred Veber: "Civilization is a cultural series shapes with major and similar cultural specifications for several specific society".

- Batomur: point of view, civilization is a cultural collection fromed by major cultural themes and similar to some particular communities.

- Herskuits: "Civilization is a series of knowledge, arts, technics, customs, establishments, and social institutions developed through inventions and innovations and activities of human group during past centuries and eras and they are prevalent in all parts of a society which have connection with each other. Like Egypt, Greece and Iran civilization".

- Civilization is things enter from one society to the other one and it is new in that society.[3]

---

1. Bros Koen (1993), 39
2. Rabbani, Rasool & Mojtaba Shahnooshi (2001), 3
3. QaraeeMoqaddam, Amanollah (1995), 150-151

Cultural Values

As we said, cultural values shapes the central part of culture for every country; however it is of worth mentioning that value concept has several meaning and different people express different ideas about it. The following definition expresses our desired meaning for cultural values in its best way. Cultural values are "governing ideas and guiding rules for thought and action" for a specific society and it is also a powerful force to shape motivations, life style and choosing the product by consumer.[1] However, the important point here is that capacity and intensity of cultural values is different from one culture to the other one. Capacity mention to this point that whether a cultural value is positive or negative, intensity shows the capability or importance of a value inside the culture. In some American cultures, for instance, respecting to elderly people has negative capacity and its intensity is average. Most of the Americans prefer youth to old people but in countries like Korea, Japan and Mexico respecting the elderly people has a positive and high capacity.[2] As Yoon (2003) said, all culture symbols reflect in different levels of radio and television, for that reason we expect that mass media programs in a social connection reflect the culture of a society. Meanwhile, programs show the way people thing, what stimulate them to show reaction, it shows people relations. Whereupon those symbols, customs and values of a culture reflect in a mass media. Through

1. Tese, et. al (1989)
2. Chan & Chang (2002), 388

usage of symbol analysis, cultural phenomenon will analyze like a language.[1]

Major Specifications of a Culture
1. Culture is not learned.
2. Culture is common among people of a society.
3. Culture is a reserve of human knowledge, which transferred from one generation to the other one.
4. Cultures are different with each other.
5. Cultures have common elements all over the world.
6. Culture is a series of life methods.[2]

What distinguishes human being from animal has four specifications originated from culture:
1. Thinking & learning power
2. Speaking
3. Technology
4. Group living.[3]

Other Specifications of Culture are as follows:
1. Culture is public but specific; it includes all human activities and every activity is a cultural action.
2. Culture is variable but stable; with regard to the chronological and locational conditions, every social phenomenon is changeable and it influence on other social phenomenon.
3. Culture is compulsory but optional; relation between person and society culture - person can do or not do an action as culture but if he does not perform it he shall observe its rules and regulations.[4]

---

1. Fisk (2007), 11
2. Qaraee Moqaddam, Amanollah (1995), 152
3. Vosooqi, Mansoor & Aliakbar NikKholgh (1999), 156
4. Rabbani, Rasool & Mojtaba Shahnooshi (1997), 41

Acculturation
- Acculturation means adoption of cultural elements of other culture.[1]
- Sometimes one culture adopts elements of other culture, which called acculturation.[2]
- Acculturation is a process that a person knows all culture backgrounds, accepts it profoundly and is being compatible with it.[3]
- Acculturation means the description of revolutions for a group culture when connecting with other group.[4]

Unilateral Acculturation
- It imposes on person unilaterally and by society.

Bilateral Acculturation
- It is about those people who emigrate from one society to the new one, which has different culture, the mutual transferring phenomenon of cultural specifications called bilateral acculturation.[5]

Sociability
- It is a process through which person becomes familiar with society norms, he learns them and execute them to live in concordance with his group and society norms.[6]

---

1. Bros Koen (1993), 59
2. *Ibid*, 44
3. QaraeeMoqaddam, Amanollah (1995), 158
4. Rabbani & Sahhnooshi (2001), 50
5. QaraeeMoqaddam, Amanollah (1995), 158
6. Vosooqi, Mansoor & Aliakbar NikKholgh (1999), 164

Cultural Norms

- A Cultural norm is in fact one of the stabilized criterions expected by a group based on its members thought and manners.[1]

- It is a permanent criterion inside a special culture, which possibly exist. Like values, customs and believes.[2]

Sub Culture or Some Culture

- Social groups like different tribes and locational and local groups and finally different social group of a society has separate and specific small culture, which is concordance with society culture, and people follow it, which called sub culture.[3]

- It belongs to a small group of society, which it also belongs to a bigger culture of society for adopting most of its norms. However, as every cultural group has its own specific norms, it separates from a bigger culture.

- In another way, they are a group of behavioral paradigms different with prevalent culture patterns but they are different simultaneously.[4]

Cultural Integration

- It is an organizational and practical integration of all elements of a culture.[5]

- Group accommodation is an effort to settle disputes resulted from continuous mutual actions and separated

---

1. Bros Koen (1993), 38
2. *Ibid*, 61
3. Vosooqi & NikKholgh (1999), 177
4. Bros Koen (1993), 40-56
5. *Ibid*, 64

mutual actions or settle down disputes among people or those who perform those actions.

- Consistency is a complete aspect of accommodation and it is that efforts that group members intentionally perform to balance between themselves and group.[1]

Cultural Aggression

- It refers to those conditions in which one culture tries to destroy other culture through genocide.[2]

Counterculture

- It depends on those groups, which intensely reject norms and expectations of the dominant culture and fight with it.[3]

Cultural Shock

- It is when a person lives among a stranger cultural environment and among people where he is not partner with their fundamental believes.[4]

Cultural Transformation

- Whenever we witness for new elements and cultural series in a culture, which leads to the transformation of its content and structure, then we encounter with a cultural transformation.[5]

---

1. QaraeeMoqaddam (1995), 168
2. Rabbani & Shahnooshi (2001), 50
3. Bros Koen (1993), 4
4. *Ibid*, 43
5. *Op. cit*

Cultural Complex

- This one comes from mixture of congruent cultural units, which shape a greater and more active unit called cultural complex.[1]

- It is a group of cultural elements attached to each other.[2]

Public Culture (folklore)

Folklore shapes from two parts; Folk meaning "public" and Lore means knowledge and information and it uses for customs uses in a specific region which are exclusive for that area.[3]

It includes customs, believes, games, dances, fictions, legends, stories, proverbs and sentences, which transferred orally and verbally. Researchers provided different ideas about historical background of Folklore word and scientific studies about public knowledge subjects. Some believe that Thoms an English antiquary in 1846 for the first time used Folklore word to mention as a knowledge, which investigates about traditions, habits and believes of public. Some researchers also believe public culture as a branch for anthropology knowledge.

The importance of public culture relates in it's popular specification and it is not born from an individual thought. It comes from routine events of people life, it transfers from one group to the other one and during this transfer, it transforms consistent with generations requirements. In order to understand the spirit of each

---

1. Vosooqi, Mansoor & AliAkbar NikKholq (1999), 180
2. Bros Koen (1993), 69
3. Qaraee Moqaddam (1995), 168

group of people, it is enough to have a little study on their folklore culture. For that reason, public literature relates in tradition works and verbal narrations with negligence and it mentions to public culture. It studies its culture origin in public songs and stories, story poems, puzzles, proverbs and dramas. Public knowledge (folklore) takes effect from human intellectual and chimerical life together with outstanding reflection of financial manifestations and his intellectual developments.

In accordance with studies of Anjavi Shirazi, public knowledge is inspiration source for poets and authors. Public knowledge of different tribes encompasses a plenty of similarities for specific subjects, most of which exist in fictions for search and study. For example: 1) proverbs; 2) fire and lighting: which is holy and for worship in all public cultures, world was in darkness since creation started and God gave it lighting. 3) Killing child: based on a Rom legend, Romoloos, Rom king is the child of Merrikh. After being born, some people try to sink him but he survives as legends and a wolf take care of him. a sample of this story exists in Shahname written by Ferdowsi, when Zal father of Rostam has white hairs when he was born, his father SAM is very angry about this deficiency as leaves him in mountains to kill him. Phoenix finds him and takes care about him. 4) Plants: they believe some plants have life giving specification. 5) Birds: ancient china people believed that Sinhu or Dorna lives one hundred year and it has munificence. 6) Iranian Myths: Sohrab comes from Rostam love in Samangan. In Chinese Myths, "Nocha" comes from transformation of a wise man called Smart Pearl.

Among narration of verbal literature and public culture exemplum, authors registered native and bizarre words as the narrator pronounced them and through voice symbols.

Ethnocentrism

It mentions to behavior, judgment, and belief that make an individual and a group superior because of their culture and ethnicity and when evaluating one of the cultural aspects of another society, they use their standard culture.[1]

Conclusion

With regard to the mentioned discussions about culture, we come to the following results:

- Culture is unity giving factor for social values
- Culture systemize human behaviors and it controls instincts
- Culture distinguishes societies from each other.
- Culture is learned. Culture transferring first performs by family and relatives group and then by other resources like organizations and circles outside the family, educational institutions, mass media and social media from society to the individuals.
- Culture is the result for human experiences, which was born and it became more complex during centuries and eras and protracted generations.
- Materialized and intellectual dimensions are continuously facing with gradual changing which manifest itself through a series and during centuries and

---

1. QaraeeMoqaddam, Amanollah (1995), 164

eras as revolutions, which distinguishes different periods of human history.

• A specific culture relates in a certain geographical area or a unique ideology, like Iranian culture or Islamic culture.

Summary

Chapter 3 considers culture definition and the subject that we do not have still a precise and comprehensive definition for Culture. Culture includes two intellectual and material parts, which agreed upon by all people. The word Culture surrounded with some definitions like "cultural awkwardness or cultural delay", "cultural aggression", "utopian culture" and cultural values. Cultural specifications, cultural norms, sub cultures, culture adoption, and sociability elaborated completely in this chapter. Public culture and folklore is also other main debates in this chapter. The major result for this chapter is that culture is a factor to unify social values, it systemizes human behavior, and it distinguishes communities from each other. It is always face with gradual changing during long years. For that reason, we shall dedicate specific emphasis over culture and factors influence on it and investigate it specifically.

Chapter 4
Oral Culture

Oral Literature

Oral literature is the intellectual heritage and fictional and non-fictional traditions, and people drama normally transfers orally from one generation to the other one. Sometimes idioms like public literature, ethnic literature and folklore literature uses for oral literature.

The importance of oral literature in people culture is very high and some countries use it instead of folklore idiom. Historically, oral literature prefers on compiled literature, because thousand years ago, before human being invent danger and to enter to his historical life, he could enjoy from speaking capability. It is not a hard job to say that people for a long period before the invention of handwriting analyzed phenomenon to find answers for their questions. Alternatively, they narrated memories of hunting or other issues to spend leisure time. They told stories about legends and they made legends. Most of the legends and proverbs created before the invention of handwriting and they transferred by language from one generation to the other one. Studies and investigations performed by anthropologists about ancient ethnics in 19th and 20th century and gathering myths and legends of some of these ethnics by investigators confirms this subject. Literature at that time registered through memory not by writing.[1]

Most of the fine literature works like Iliad and Odise were prevalent among people orally before writing. Khares Mobtelni besides giving legendary - romantic description called Zoryadres and Odatis, emphasis that this legend is very prevalent among people. During next years and through changing and transforming, these legends changed to Goshtasb and Ketmayoon in Shahname.[2] The oldest oral literature text of Iran, which is accessible today, is Gahani or Gasheha, which beside Veda, Gilgamesh and Torat, is the oldest world literal texts.

The first imagination for the most ancient type of Iran literature, in fact, relates in a series of religious and ethnic legends, which has different indices for recognizing them as oral works. These indices relates in the making of these legends, which proved through archeological and historical studies.[3]

Specifications of Oral Literature

Through studying about oral literature of different nations and ethnics during recent one hundred years, it led investigators to the conclusion that oral literature holds general specifications based of which we can distinguish the said literature from compiled literature. Here are the specifications for oral literature:

---

1. Chadvik, Preamble, VII
2. Tafazolli, 18-19
3. Moazen, 17

A) **Unknown Author:** Oral subjects in contrast with compiled works, which comes from a creative mind of certain people, have not obvious and certain compiler. None of the legends common among our people and even most of the public literature traditional stories like Samk Ayar which we have their written form, have not a certain compiler. At its best condition, they mention to the collector name or their reporter in introduction or text of book. In Samk Ayar, for example, someone called "Sadaqatebne Abelqasem" is narrator and "Faramarzebne Khodadadebne Abdollah" also introduces himself as author or book collector.[1]

Oral literature, in fact, has been always changing and transforming and it always consisted itself with social and political context of the related era. Those sections harmonized with the related era spirit, preserved and the residue, which did not reflect the time related spirit, destroyed.[2] Narrations of each era express the spirit and public conscious of that time. We can describe this subject as this, narrators for each period in contrast with plenty of subjects they had in mind, and however, in special conditions and situations, they chose those narrations, which had more correspondence with that time spirit. In preamble of Stories of Mashdi Galin Khanom, we see that she memorized a plenty of legends most of them recorded and wrote by Alool Satan. Through a glance over Mashdi Galin Khanom legends, we understand that legends with topics of commerce and business dedicate the

---

1. Arjani (2006), 1/1-3/4
2. Khaliqi (1977), 25

majority to themselves. As social values of Iran was changing at that time, capital element and commercial capital held special role in society and it was a criterion to distinguish social base of individuals.[1]

B) Transforming Method: In contrast with compiled literature, the main form of transforming oral literature from one generation to other one is orally. This issue paves the way to shaping of different and several types of a certain narration like Legend, Epigram, Quatrain and Song. It is unlikely to find two completely similar narrations; for Rostam and Sohrab; for example, we have three different narrations by one narrator.[2] These narrations are similar just in general ideas. Narrator in fact, improvises the real theme of the same story in another shape and he adds branches for it.[3]

One of the reasons for providing different narrations is geographical and living, political and cultural differences. Citing to this point, Abdolnabi Fakhrozamani, describes storytelling differences among "Iranian, Turonian and Indian people".[4]

C) Repetition: is another specification of oral subjects. For many cases, we witness for similar events by different people.[5] In one of the narrations entitled in "angels of apple tree" recorded in Neishaboor, legend hero encounters with three-slept devil for three times. Each time he awakes them and the kills them with sword.

---

1. Mesbahipoor, 82
2. Zariri (1990), 391-408
3. Khaleqi, *Hamase*, 69
4. Taraz, 22-24; Mahjoob, *Op.cit*
5. Kalvino, 50

The method for awaking devils and killing them is similar but narrator expresses the details repeatedly.[1] On the other hand, in another narration, for example entitled "adventures of two sisters" (Nay, discloses the secret of a crime). Narrator talks about one certain poem repeatedly instead of legend characters.[2] Most stories and narrations have different usages besides repetition theme, or cliché phrases.

D) Language: is another specification for oral literature. This is the same conversational language, the live language people talk with it in markets to have routine communication. For those reason different descriptions, combinations, and individual substances entered in written and poem works most of which do not exist in official literal language[3] and surely we do not see them in Persian cultures. Some of these words and combinations dates back to the interval period of Persian language which still people use them in different Persian accents all over the Iran, like Aras means tear, "Beig or Beheig" means bride, "Anjidan" means whispering.[4] Another specification of this language, which distinguishes it from official polite language, is the little usage of words and arabic combinations. There is less trace of speech decoration with proverbs, news, verses, single substances, scientific combinations and arabic literature[5] and generally it has a more fluent and attractive language.

Another lingual specification of oral literature is the tendency toward fluency or frankness. This frankness makes the usage of plenty of descriptions and words that

1. Khazaee, 121-125
2. JafariQanavati (2003), 134-139
3. Safa, 1/16
4. Qeysari (2010), 18
5. Safa, "notes 2002", 2/772

are "vulgar", "obscene" and "unethical". However the reality is that public people intend allegory by using these words. The issue faced with critic and allegory, in fact is transferring oral language fluency to written language and this is the subject that official literature rejects it and fight with it that is it likes politeness. What makes the language tendency toward fluency is the specific situation of speaker and audience, because what people say always has meaning and conception with having the real condition for speaking and through the nearest social situation for speaking.[1]

E) Entertaining: is one of the specifications for oral literature to entertain listener and audience, refreshment, make listeners happy and programming for leisure times. Fiction telling and other narration types, singing local songs in winter ceremonies, common in recent past,[2] performance of game show and narration of riddles are some examples. In Arak the idiom, "Shoqat" (means speech or night entertainment) uses for narrations[3] supervise over this specification. Heroic poem and similar stories also narrated for entertainment and amusement of courtiers.[4]

Although priority of oral literature over compiled literature historically is a public and global subject however, making comparison between Iran and other communities confirms the depth root of oral tradition in our land, which has different reasons. Oral tradition is a specification dedicated to nomadic people;[5] when for stable civilizations

---

1. Todorf, 89-90
2. Anjavi, 1/65-70
3. Naderi & Movahedi (2001), 4
4. Chadvik, 144/I: 21
5. Amoozegar, 324

like Mesopotamia and Egypt which had stable life, writing tradition had more importance.

In contrast with this respectful old oral tradition with depth root of Iranian culture and its permanent influences over official and compiled literature, division idea increased in our official literature during past one thousand years and for different reasons and it continues today. Public literature which official and university assemblies use it, in fact, monitors over valuation by the users of this idiom. In fact, most authors believe public literature as without depth root.

Similarities and Differences of Oral Literature for Different Ethnics and Nations

Oral literature of different ethnics and nations enjoys from certain similarities and differences. The existing similarities have two reasons:

They relate to the fundamental commons of human being. Most needs of people are similar. During fighting against natural and social problems, they acquire common experiences. Through investigation about ancient tribes, Henry Morgan, concluded that human being experience passed from straight roads and people necessities in similar situations had one base. These common experiences pave the ground for flourishing of somehow common talents. Mah Pishooni (Moon Forehead), Bolbole Sargashte (Wondered Nightingle) and hundreds of other narrations registered among Hindu-European ethnics.[1] In addition we here mention to the invulnerable theme exists among

---

1. Arne-Thampson, 256, 354 - 355

some of the sagas of these ethnics. Investigators assign the similarities existing among oral literature of other ethnics to the common ancestors. However, besides these ethnics, we witness for remarkable similarities among oral literature of other ethnics living thousands kilometer far from each other without historical common points. Some of our national saga stories like Rostam & Sohrab, Akouan Devil & Rostam & Esfandyar & White Devil have many similarities with some of the ancient Chinese fictions.[1] Here Indians have fictions called "sorrow of the flying bird"[2] which has surprising homology with one of the Iranian fictions called "golden forelock and pearl teeth" and there are several narrations for it in different parts of Iran.[3]

However, the next reason for these similarities relates in relations and conflicts among ethnics and nations. The existence of several wars led to the captivity of a plenty of soldiers groups, occupation of one land by another ethnic and emigration and residence of some parts of the victor ethnic to that land and compulsory emigration during history.

Commercial relations are cases led to the marriage of cultures and transferring of oral literature of an ethnic to other land. Iran history is a good witness for these generalities.

Oral literatures of different ethnics have major differences with each other. This issue depends on several

---

1. Kuyaji, 3-13
2. Deriken (2004), 360-367
3. Anjavi, 140

factors including geographical disputes, differences in life style and difference for nature controlling or civilization level difference. Some of these difference factors have fundamental role in civilization level. For that reason, oral literature of nomadic ethnics who live in tribe has outstanding differences with ancient Iranian civilization. Veladimir Prab mentioned to some parts of these differences related in ancient civilizations.[1] As this issue is important, here we mention to these differences:

A) Content Variety: investigation about narration contents for ancient ethnics shows that most of them have mythical specifications, when oral literature of some nations like Iran has been very variable and it includes several types.

B) Reading and Writing: in oral literature, nations who enjoy from old civilization, knowledge subject, public reading and writing, book and book reading has great feedback. An important part of Iran and Greece myths, for instance, compiled by great poets who transformed to myth after this national action and their names became eternal in history and people minds. This is a subject poets had information about it: I will not die, I am alive, and I distributed speaking seed.[2] Although ancient ethnics myths gathered with more delay, however, author, writer and especially poet enjoys from a great location in oral literature of nations holding ancient civilization. In part of Odise when one poet and one druid fell down in front of Odise and wants him not to kill them, Odise kills druid but

1. Roots, 197
2. Ferdowsi, 288

calls off to kill poet. Hemer believes that "he afraid to kill a man who learned a holy art by Gods, so this poet had influence over kingdom not bishop or druid... .[1]

C) Political Organization of Society: government structure for tribe communities has simple hierarchy. In these societies, one person is the boss or there is a council formed by elderly (like Indian tribes; cf.: Mid: 148). This subject reflected completely in ancient ethnics fictions;[2] however among Iranian fictions, we encounter with a society, which has a complex governmental structure; king, great minister, left and right ministers, princess, and hero are examples of this complex. Among Iranian fictions, we face with other characters like Judge, inspector, writer, etc... .[3]

D) Social Division of Job: One of the differences of ancient communities with societies with ancient civilization is the amount and expansion of social division of job. Among recent communities, normally occupations and different jobs performs professionally by different people and groups. This issue naturally reflects in literal creations of these communities. Among Iranian fictions, the existence of characters like; cobble, black smith, carpenter and tailor is an axiomatic subject, but we do not observe jobs variety among fictions related in ancient ethnics. Alternatively, there is a very limited variety.

E) The Quality of Having Relation with Nature: The important and outstanding specification of verbal

---

1. Hamilton, 19
2. Deriken (2004), 79
3. Anjavi (1973), *Stories*, 71

literature for ancient tribe is their tendency toward nature, which is visible among their fictions, myths, and roots from their relation with nature. Life style of ancient tribes has relation with their living location. The more nomadic, the more taking influence from nature Indians, for instance, especially those living in North America depended on hunting and fishing because of shortage of plant covering in their living place. Some of them, not also for foods provision but also for preparing their clothes, home and tabernacle and even their jewelry depended on buffalo hunting.[1] For them, life starting and implementation had firm relation with hunting and drought and famine.

Nature and life style had also influence on husband selection. In one fiction, a mother says, "my daughter shall marry with a hunter to compensate all shortages of our life".[2] The reflection of this subject is also visible in poems of Indians for the description of positive specifications of their heroes: He was my son, brave and without fear. He was a great hunter. He was a great artist.[3]

Nature loving, creatures, and hunting animals even reflected in people names and innuendo. Indians tribes bosses, for example had titles like "Gray fox," "Blue Snake" and "Wolf". These names exist among nomadic Arabians. Among Hoor Arabs in South Arab names like Jahish (foal), Khenzir (boar), Zabe (hyena) is not abnormal.[4] This subject is considerable through the

1. Mid, 123
2. Deriken (2004), 102
3. *Ibid*, 295
4. Tesijer, 60

reflection angle of Totemi believes in fictions. Fictions of nomadic ethnic, in fact, is the existence of more naked Totemi believes, when we shall distinguish these believes thorough scrutinizing in nation fictions.

In contrast with these nature loving, Iranian fictions and myths pay attention to human being. On the other hand, heroes of Iranian myths and fictions, in their best situation are kings, princesses, and heroes with a complete human appearance. In these myths and fictions, human being is not a weak creature against nature. After sudden discovery of fire, he separates iron from granite with fire and then he uses forging;[1] then he performs farming, a profession that needs irrigation in a country like Iran and it demands special organizing. For that reason, he plans to change natureand constructs home and hygiene facilities like "bathroom and huge palaces".[2] All of these are civilization signs and we do not see them among myths and fictions of nomadic tribes.

Social Rituals and Oral Literature

Oral literature in every society has direct relation with social ceremonies and rituals. Outstanding majority of these ceremonies hold their specific literature. This issue is so important that made some people like Frizer to go toward excess. In most sections of his book, Frizer continuously tries to prove that every mythical narration has relation with agriculture to conclude that through centuries, myths leaves rituals, and goes independently among oral tradition and finally changes to different types of oral literature.

---

1. Ferdowsi, 1/29-31
2. Ibid, 1/43-44

Rituals and different ceremonies for every ethnic and nation called "Customm Folklore" and it divides to three parts of calendar folklore, mourning folklore and happiness folklore. Calendar folklore is a series of ceremonies hold in certain date every year. Mourning and happiness folklore is also reunions families implement for their sorrows and happiness (cf.: folklore culture). Among these three parts, calendar folklore and its literature is much expanded and diverse among Iranian society. Ceremonies hold based on solar calendar roots in believes before islam iranian people, like Norooz, Sade, Yalda, Rain Demanding Ceremonies, Shark Ceremonies, Crop Ceremonies, etc... moon calendar ceremonies also relates in islamic believes like Ramazān, Moharram, Eyde Ghorban, Fetr, etc... . the important point here is the interruption of many Iranian customs of before Islam with Islamic believes like reading special pray for NewYear changing moment in Norooz or holding Nazri Sofre which relates in the Iranian culture before Islam.[1] However some of them completely coincide with Islamic believes. Calendar customs and ceremonies of Iranian people holds together with different oral literature.

Interaction of Oral Literature with Official Literature

Between oral and written literature always has been a mutual or more precisely an interaction. Most likely, the first written literature texts prepared from oral narrations. The oldest literal texts like Gilkamesh, Veda, Avesta, narrated orally before changing to written form. Most of the world written literature masterpieces directly or

---

1. Foji Moto, 185

indirectly adapted from oral literature. Biowolf, for instance, directly written based on oral literature[1] and Shahname by Ferdowsi has written with two interceders from oral literature.[2] Some of the fictions and stories of Mathnavi Manavi like Tarmaz Joker or Joohi[3] and all ManaqebolarefIn have oral origin.

Writing narrations had determining influence for their preservation and maintenance against smashing up. Some of these books which took influence by oral literature used by a lot of people or in schools as the main books or auxiliary or for winter soirees[4] came to oral culture again, for that reason they were the subject for oral narration of people. Bedoone Mathnavi, for instance most of the today's fictions could not find a new life higher than written literature.[5]

Among Iranian society before and after Islam, one of the prevalent themes was that a country will develop through good wills of its king, otherwise, the country will ruin.[6] Based on this thought, there are some fictions in many narrations titles "Niyate Padeshah" and Shahname holds its oldest one. For such case, Bahrame Goor inevitably sleeps in a village home. Because of what homeowner said, he decides to be a bad man against people. Morning when woman tries to milk cow, she sees there is no milk in cow. She says to her husband: king's intention has changed. Bahram asked: Why do you say so? Woman said: when king goes cruel, wealth goes out

1. Chadvik, 556-558
2. Khaleqi (2007), 7
3. Zarrinkoob (1366), *Bahr Dar Kouzeh*, 281-285
4. Anjavi (2000), *Ceremonies*, 661; Moayyed Mohseni, 341
5. Martself, 71
6. Raqeb, 162

from society. "Milk will dry in boobies," then Bahram changed his will and again cow had a lot of milk.[1]

As it is obvious not all these oral and written narrations have theme differences with each other and the little difference is just for their appearances. At the end of all these oral and written narrations, there is one sentence with this conception, when king has bad will; it has bad influence on daily life of people. This subject expresses the unity and harmony of thought and ideas in our official and non - official culture against king or the political power.

Different Types of Oral Literature

Goal and subject of our discussion for different literature is categorization of literal works. This work facilitates the subject of literal works criticism and their recognition.[2] Since long time ago, in Iran, literature divided in two general types of poem and prose and then without paying special attention to prose, they concentrate their discussion on poem; poems also categorized based on their types, like: Mathnavi, Ode and sonnet. What has ignored here is the meaning and materials forming the literal works. This type of categorization copied from Arab literature,[3] are among the most non - scientific types of literal works,[4] because poem and prose cannot be distinguished from each other.[5]

The problem is not this type of categorization. The second problem is the past scholars concentration on technics and precise of poem and poets, poem palinode and

---

1. Ferdowsi, 468-470
2. Shafiee, 97-98
3. *Op.cit*
4. Shamisa (1991), 38-39
5. Khanlari (1972), 474

its details and simultaneously not paying attention to literal prose. a general look over books written about literal science among Iran literature history, like: almoᶜjam Shams Qeis Razi or Arazatolᶜroozayn[1] all confirm this issue.

The main reason for not paying attention to the literal prose and considering poem secrets have been the complete and autocratic sovereign of poem over our official literature and culture during the past 10 centuries. This issue becomes clearer when we see that "the kings of Persian literature in global culture are poem, not prosaic".[2] Mastery of poem over prose demands special cultural, social and political grounds provided by continuous aggressions of foreigners; aggressions which were together with murdering, blooding and loot. Prose talks about wisdom and it needs reasoning, when poem is the most suitable form to express emotions and feeling and it does not demand reasoning.

Two points are important when considering oral literature in Iran:

1. In contrast to old theories, today we cannot separate different literal works completely, because they have influence on each other and it might be that this influence leads to the formation of new types.[3]

2. Although literature theory including "different literal works" are global and public debates, however, we shall pay attention that different cultures enjoy from different public narrations;[4] Hero type, for instance, does not exist among some ethnics, because it needs a society with dynamic economy and culture to have a powerful,

1. Safa (1972), *Tarikh Adabyate dar Iran*, 298
2. Mojtaba, 121
3. Volk, 244 -245
4. Dandes (1974), 17

triumph, fighter and aristocracy bed, so it can manifest itself as kings and brave heroes in this literal type.[1]

Some of the oral literature types stay in one group because they have common aspects with each other, like different types of narration or Fiction including: Myth, Legend and Epigram. Alternatively different drama literature like: naghali, passion play, pardekhani, takhte hozi, sokhanvari and female games. The next part like minstrelsy, passion, screen reading, flat pool, eloquence, couplet, and ballad are in oral poems group. Other types like puzzle, prayer, and curse are not in this group and they do not have common aspects with each other. In addition to drama and story literature, some researchers talk about the subtitle of nonfiction literature and they dedicate this for those without special group. For that reason, "nonfiction literature" as they believe includes poem, proverb, puzzle, josh, word and innuendo.[2]

A) Fiction: It mentions to those works that have the imaginative specification besides "story" Therefore, it has the second name of "narration literature". Some of the literal investigators just dedicate prose stories to fiction literature.[3] Based on their idea, lyrics and festive poems like Veis & Ramin, by Fakhroddin Asᶜad Gorgani & Khosro & Shirin by Nezami are not in this group. However, other investigators believe that all fictions including prose and poem exist in Fiction.[4]

---

1. Bahar, Mehrdad, 372-373
2. Blokbashi (2009), 172
3. Mirsadeqi, 21; Kaden, 270-271
4. Broeein (2003), 29; Barahani (1983), 40

The main part of Persian fiction literature among official or compiled literature has poem type and as we mentioned earlier, in its real concept, prose means imaginative one which is very rare in the official literature of old Iran; Even books like: MarzbanName, Faraedolsolook & Kelile & Demne although have different subjects but they are closer to official prose. Their goal is teaching in different subjects and they are far from imagination as the specification for fiction literature. Most of these works are not even entertaining. This position is completely different in oral fiction literature, first because the main part of fiction literature in oral literature field is in prose type and we cannot make comparison between poem fictions with prose ones in quantity aspect. The second reason is that the emotional, imaginative and artistic aspects in oral fictions are more powerful and the main goal of fiction writer is to amuse and motivate passion and surprise reader and listener. If he aims for training and philosophical ideas, he puts them in other grades.[1]

1. Legend: it is among the important oral literature which has been prevalent among all ethnics and nations from long times ago. Some call it as the most famous and popular type of oral literature.[2] This type of literature had a lot of role in spiritual life of people.[3] There are different idioms for fiction in different regions of Iran like "Osane" and "Osone" in Khorasan and parts of Mazandaran, "Tale" in Shiraz and south part of Iran, "Shoqat" in Arak.

---

1. Mahjoob (2008), *Literature*, 50
2. Rahmani (1995), *afsanehaye dari*, 41
3. Asrari, 214

2. Myth: Owing to mythological, there are a lot of anthropology and folkloric studies especially studies about the nomadic communities, which their myths are alive, and they bring about a clear-cut understanding about myth. In accordance with these studies, myths hold holy believes of people in special step of social evolution.[1] These holy believes in fact narrates the creation and start of a phenomenon. The active persons in these narrations are extraordinary creation.[2] For that reason, we can say that, myth for the ancient man is his religion and spiritual wealth.[3] Through analyzing myths, we can understand believes and class forms of ancient ethnics and the reason for their social, cultural, and mental behaviors.[4]

3. Tale: it is of worth reminding that among Iranian scholars and critics, the word story, fiction and narration more or less have similar meaning and they are synonyms. It is the same in dictionaries. Especially when we talk about narration works of oral literature and the past Persian literature, it comes true more. Here we use the word Tale to call a specific type of narration and to separate it from other narration types. What we mean by word Tale is a special type of different narrations in oral and written literature with religious content, which narrate for giving advice together with promulgation of religious thoughts.

---

1. Bahar, Mehrdad (2002), 371
2. Alyadeh, 11
3. Esmaeelpoor (1999)
4. *Ibid*, 16-19

4. Anecdote (cf.: Tale): there are narrations about historical characters, events and geographical names in oral literature, which have news - story aspect and in narration point of view, they are real and true. Although it might be that, they are not real;[1] like issues about life of Hafez or contents of the first volume of Ferdowsi Name about Ferdowsi by people. These texts called anecdote (Tale), (Anjavi). Among other samples are anecdotes in Manaqebolarefin about Molavi family and about Barmaki family in history books.[2] Anecdote is different with other oral literature types, because the news and information is more important in anecdote, in another way; anecdote has a more imaginative aspect. Its structure is also different with other narration types. Tajik investigators use "Narrative" for anecdote. As narrative has very different meaning in our oral and written language, so it cannot be a precise idiom.

5. Epigram: one of the most prevalent types of oral literature of Iranian people is Epigram. Today most family sessions enjoy from telling epigrams. People love epigraming and making epigrams even for serious social issues and phenomenon and as one of the Iran experts believe, Iranian people are the most lovers of this literal type.[3]

B) Dramatic literature: In official literature and culture of Iran, there has not been drama and dramatic literature. Beizaee, mentions to some of the reasons for it (22-23); however there have been regulations in people culture in dramatic type. These performances had the main specifications for play like simulation, using masks, adding games and persuading actions to speech and

---

1. Rahmani, 93-94
2. Sajjadi, 173, 184, 242-23
3. Sipek, 83

concluding dramatic contract.[1] These dramas had their own specific literature, which actors talked about them. However, because this was not a written literature and it transferred like culture parts by generations, for that reason, there were different narrations about it among people. Their texts also changed simultaneous with social revolutions. Beside these regulations, there were other dramas performed with other goals like narration. The recent dramas had not even and occasional aspect and they could perform it in different times.

1. Narration: it is an arabic word means, someone who is very narrating, dislocates, transferable, movable and quick horse.[2] In addition, most likely it came to persian language during Qajar period. Narration is a part of a more developed phenomenon called "story enactment".[3]

2. Curtain Reading: it is a type of tale reading with using a pictorial curtain and it has more dramatic aspects than other types of story - telling. Subjects for stories, which curtain reader performs the, are mostly about Imam Hossein and his followers martyrdom in Karbala, which called "main" sessions; However sub-sessions like Zamene Ahoo, the attendance of Imam Reza in Maemoon session, the curtain reader has other names like: Dervish or Mentor.

3. Threnoding: this is a specific shape of narrating miseries of religious Imams especially Imam Hossein (peace be upon him) through sad emotions and make audiences to cry. Its root like what it is today dates back to Safaviye period. There is no doubt that it finds its root in book called *Roozatolshohada* compiled by Vaez

---

1. Beizaee (1965), 29
2. Qayyem, 1135
3. Safa, *eshare*, 463

Kashefi.[1] This book complied simultaneous with officially recognition of Shiite religion in Iran.

4. Macebearer telling: macebearer is a Turkish word, which in *Asraroltohid*, Poetical Work of Moezzi and Khaghani and *Khosro & Shirin* means commander for army. In poetical work of Anvari, Mathnavi Maenavi, and Shams Generalities, it means ceremonies boss and footman and finally in Borhane Qate, Anendraj Dictionary and Saadi kolyat it means group commander and caravan fugleman.[2]

5. Women Shows: this part mentions to those shows hold exclusively for women and men could not enter the show. In these games, the most serious issues narrated through humorous and irony language. Humor and laughing have been the most original specifications of these games. If they needed a man for their shows, a woman played that role as man, she had a masculine face with a mild grim. Content of these games are a combination of prose and poem. Their language is broken conversation like, "I love you my aunt, I adore you, I am the fire on the top of your hookah, and I am the sun at the edge of your roof".[3] They used Def, Tombak and Dayereh for these games. Some female musicians sometimes took the responsibility to perform show against receiving a certain wage.[4]

6. Ashiqha: they are huckster musicians and singers who play with their musical instruments or sing in public places like coffeehouses and ceremonies. The word "Ashiq" became prevalent from 9th century. Ashiqi literature divides in two general types: one stories and second poems and

---

1. Chelkofski, 101
2. Yousefi (1991), 5
3. Anjavi (1973), *baziha*, 14
4. MoayyedMohseni, 156

lyrics. Stories have two types: one epic or heroic and amorously or lyrical. Koroghloo, Ghachagh Karam, Shah Esmaeel and Arab Zangi, and Main and Karam stories are examples for the two groups respectively.

7. **Poem Telling:** Sher (Poem) in Baloochestan pronounces as "Shear" or "Shayr". Here Poet or Shaer is not someone who tells poet but he is someone who performs "Shear" together with musical instruments and singing.[1] Baluch said the poet hero[2].

8. **Shahname Reading:** It is reading Shahname from text with special voice among crowd of people. Based on covert to some couplets of Shahname, some investigators date back Shahname Reading to the age of Shahname.[3]

c) **Different Independent genres:** Independent types are not either fiction literature or dramatic literature:

1. **Poem:** we did not receive poems for ancient Persian language from west and south west of Iran during Medians or Archimedeans. Our information about poems belongs to Median Iran period especially Median Part and Pars is more than other periods. From somehow long period of Ashkanian, we just have Zeriran and Asoorik Tree, which of course they interpolated and changed to a mixture of Median part and pars.[4]

2. **Conundrum:** It mentions to the two forms of poem and prose which speaker talks about specifications of a phenomenon through body language. He asks its audience to reply.

---

1. Boostan (1991), 53
2. Eftekhari (1996) 12
3. Aydenloo (2008) 75
4. Esmaeelpoor (1998), 111

3. Puzzle: it means covered, silent and mute, ambiguous and insensible. For that reason, puzzle is something, which expresses the meaning or a certain name through calculation of Abjad letters or by distortion and concealing so "just a knowledgeable mind and thinking a lot can discover its secret and truth".[1] The puzzle teller in fact, bewilders the audience.

4. Proverbs and Gnomes: the speaker tells them aiming to give advice and through using literal tools in short sentence in poem or prose form. In conversational language and even in written language, proverb changes wrongly to "Byworde".

5. Words Written on Cars: these are new types of oral literature which generalized after popular usage of cars in Iran and in some of the neighborhood countries. These are a series of prose and poem texts written on external part or some of the internal part of cars.

6. Texts on Graves: expresses the culture of respecting the dead people and their commemoration. Each one has concepts and in addition to reflecting people believes in a historical period, they manifest a kind of imitation from shape and works of other historical periods.[2]

7. Mementos and Wall Writings: this is an old practice, kings and public people wrote them as mementos.

8. Texts Written on Devices: it is texts written on battle - axe, dervish crown, def, mirror case.

9. Oath, Pray Curse and Insult.

D) Children Literature: It is one part of oral literature created by elderlies, but its major part with the exception of lullaby by the participation of children. Its main goal is

---

1. Shamse Qeis, 430; Yousefi (1992), 114
2. Shayestefar, 80

teaching about different subjects especially language teaching, talent training and body training.[1]

1. Lullabies: these are songs, which mother sings in order to tranquilize her child and make him/ her sleep, with rhythms and canorous.[2]

2. Coddling and fondling songs: in contrast to lullaby, this one is to wake up child and make him/her happy. It has a quick rhythm and makes child to participate in it by shaking his hands and legs and finally codding and fondling songs are different with each other.[3]

3. Song - Playing: this one relates in children after age 2, that is when child can speak.[4] The outstanding specification of these songs is that they integrate with playing and an active contribution of child.

4. Proverb: it is a special type of children fictions, in which they narrate a short and simple story (Arne - Thompson: 1026).

Language

Based on the view point of Vorf and Saiper, language is the main core of culture. They know language as the fundamental tools for understanding human being behavior. By language, we can understand people views about their living environment events and methods they use to analyze and describe them. Whereupon, through investigation of language in different communities, cultural anthropologists can acquire more knowledge

---

1. Asrari, 272-273
2. Anjavi (1992), *Gozari*, 32-33
3. Homayooni, 56
4. Ghezel Ayagh, 128

about a special ethnic, their thinking methods and their world views and to have a more suitable description and analyzing for them. In another way, it is through analyzing of community language, which we can acquire information about culture and thinking method of that community and then consider its influence on language.[1] Worf provided hypothesis for language relativism provided in 1956. He believes that conceptions type and our understanding take influence from special language (s), which we call it, Speech. Therefore, people who talk with different languages comprehend world in different way. Language, in fact, language can reflect distinguishes which are important for people of one culture.[2]

Based on view point of SooSoor, language is a system for signs, which express meaning or thoughts.[3] Loui Straous knows language as the most important cultural phenomenon. He says, linguistic can find the major methods to investigate about integration of different factors which lead to the formation of cultural system.

Language, especially through a comprehending meaningful system, is the most important communicational tools for social interaction. In addition, language is the most prevalent common identity element, which can take the responsibility to transfer many ideas, values, and common believes in social interaction outside of geographical dimensions and land connections among different generations. Therefore, among identity

---

1. QaraeeMoqadam (2003), 84
2. *Ibid*, 87
3. Tavasolli (1992), 87

elements, language holds the first rank in social interaction and communicational network.

Dialectic Culture

It is a type of dictionary for a language, which elaborates on words descriptions, and phrases of local dialects. Every community can have different accents. The current Persian language beside the branches of "old languages" and "median languages" is one of the branches for Iranian languages, which take its root from Hindu-European languages. It is possible to divide old languages into two Avesta and Ancient Persian. Pahlavi, Parti, Soghdi, Kharazmi and Khotani are among Median languages. The current persian language is in fact a evolutional form of median/pahlavi persian language which was the language of Sasanians and it owes to some Parthian words- language of Ashkanian period.

Hamze Esfahani, Iranian, scholar, lexicologist who wrote history in arabic language writes in *Altanbih* book, that Iranian people had five languages, Pahlavi, Dari, Farsi, Khoozi and Seryani. among accent/dialectic, Soghdi was prevalent in Soghdiana. During the first Hijri centuries, Tokhari accent was prevalent in a region between Balkh and Badakhshan. Kharazmi accent also was prevalent in the first Hijri centuries. At the same time, Tabari, Kordish, Azari, Khoozi and Pars (attributed to Velayate Fars) and Razi (attributed to Rey) were prevalent. During centuries, some of these accents disappeared and some of them continued to their living.

The current Persian language, in addition to Dari, includes Arian accents of Iran for today and neighbor countries like, Kurdish, Balochi, Pashto, Tati and Asci. These accents divides based on acoustic, grammatical and lexical similarities and differences in two west and east groups, accents for Caspian Sea region (Mazandarani, Gilaki, Taleshi), central accents of Iran and Lori, Tajik Farsi from west group and Pamir Plateau accents which is prevalent in Afghanistan (Ormoori, Shaqnani and …) are among east group. The existence of original Persian words in some accents like, beaches of Persian Gulf and Balochi confirms that, these accents kept some part of old words treasure with themselves.

Structuralism Approach

This approach helps us to understand that, different social and cultural systems, which give meaning to our life, are not random and separated; they are similar to each other. Language, myths and the symbolized system is the central attention point of structuralism followers. This is because the method, which organizes its society and methods, which members have to comprehend them and their social experiences, leads in unique views.[1]

In this approach, culture is like language. Structuralism intensely takes influence from works created in structuralism linguist. Concentration of structuralism approaches toward culture depends on the recognition of allegorical elements (signs and concepts) and discovering

---

1. Fisk, 195-196

of a method, which organizes these elements in order to send a message. With regard to this process, it sometimes recognizes as an affair, which leads to decoding of semiotic processes.[1]

With regard to structuralism and culture, Lai (1999) believes that structuralism empowers us to read texts and culture formed by signs. Structuralism through semiotic leads us to see everything like a text shaped with signs which is in accordance with meaningful contracts and has systemized relational prototypes. Here we can analyze texts as they manifest codes and contracts of culture; in addition, it is possible to read texts as the ways to understand meaningful structures of cultures.

Although semiotic and structuralism uses instead of each other and on the other hand some scholars dedicate special distinguish between structuralism and semiotic. However based on the view point of this article supervisor, structuralism is a theoretical method and a general paradigm which we use it to study internal parts of culture like a text and semiotic is a methodology and technic to study and discover the meaning concealed in the fundamental layers of texts in their public meaning.

Semiology

The main studying scope of Soosoor was linguistic with limited meaning. However, after his death, his theories used as a general approach for language and meaning, it gave us a manifestation model usable for an expanded range of words and cultural actions. This general

---

1. Smith (2004)

approach studies cultural signs and culture as a type of language, now uses generally under the title of semiotic.[1]

The starting point of Soosoor discussion, is the definition for structuralized linguistic, therefore, he begins his speech in article entitled in "Basics of structuralism in Linguistic" through bringing about the difference between language (abstract-social part of language) and speech (practical-experiencing part of language). As Soosoor believes, language (abstract part) is the social part of speaking power and it is independent from person. Because person cannot individually create it or change it, language comes to existence because of the contract among members of a society.[2] He believes that linguistics shall study language and this subject shall be their concentration point for their analysis and the basis for their relation.

However, speech defines based on language: speech is the real shape of speaking power which language makes it possible. Speech is a series of linguistic units manifest itself through speaking and writing. We cannot study speech as a special, small, and historical issue. Speech organizes the witnesses for fundamental structure.[3]

As semiology deals with whatever called as sign and as approximately everything can be a sign (that is something replaced with something else), semiology shows itself as a kind of prevalent knowledge, usable in all recognition scopes. Therefore we use it to criticize beautiful arts, literature, movie and public stories and for

---

1. Hall (2003)
2. Soosoor (2001)
3. *Ibid*, 130

architecture description, to study fashion, to analyze face forms, to describe magazines and advertisements and commercial advertisements of radio and television, for medical and many other sections.[1]

Rollan Baret from 1954 up to 1956, published short articles in modern literature magazine. These articles paid attention to different parts of daily life and culture of people. His articles published on 1957 in a book named "Mythologies" which is the most important books of Baret. What made these articles different with other articles about culture, was his writing method, which made him powerful to define everything from washing machine powder and face powder called Gereta Garbo, the reaction of literal community with poem and poets for children, Eifel Tower, Crooked Ship and Toys.[2]

Through using these activities and objects as signs like a language, which transfers, meaning used his semiology approach for reading public culture.[3] In this work Baret tries to read advertisement for washing machine powder like language that is like a reasonable system, which has its own special grammar. Baret book, called "Myth in Present time" has a long article, which is a summarized description for theoretical results of analysis, which forms the most part of the main text.[4]

In semiology system of Baret, denotative is meaning and shape and guided is concept and it refers to denotative sign. For that reason, Baret changes the famous Soosoor formula, that is denotative, guided, sign

---

1. Asaberger (2006), 91
2. Abazari (2001)
3. Hall (2003), 36
4. Milenz & Bravit (2004)

as this; meaning/shape/concept/denotation. Here we shall pay attention that the sign for the first system changes to the denotation for the second system, a denotation that is meaning and shape. Conception location in the second formula is the same as guided in the first formula and the denotation follows the same rule. We can continue this to infinity. Baret in his next book uses the semiology elements of the word "denotation" instead of the first denotation; he uses the implied denotation instead of the secondary denotation. Baret claims that myth comes from the secondary denotation level; therefore, myth for semiology system is in the second rank.[1]

Baret mythologies and his method, as Abazari believes, are the inspiration source of many of the culture investigators.

Summary

Chapter 4 specifically considers oral culture. The importance of oral literature in public culture is as much as in some countries use it instead of folklore. Based on history, oral literature prefers on compiled literature, because thousand years ago, before the invention of handwriting, and entrance in its historical life, human being started speaking. It is not a hard job to say that human beings during long periods before the invention of handwriting analyzed phenomenon to reply to their questions. In addition, they talked about their hunting memories through fictions. most of the fictions and

---

1. Abazari (2001)

proverbs, in fact, created before the invention of handwriting and they transferred through language from one generation to the other one. The first imagination for the most ancient type of Iran literature is in fact the series of religious and ethnic fictions, which have different indices for calling them as oral. This chapter, in fact confirms that the oral literature and especially, language is the reason to produce and distribute culture. Studies and investigations performed by anthropologists performed in 19 and 20 century about the ancient ethnics and collecting myths and fictions of some of these ethnics by investigators confirms this claim. Literature at that time, in fact kept through memory not by writing and this increases its importance. One of the lingual specifications of the oral literature is its tendency toward fluency, which uses many definitions and words. Oral literature has many relations with people socialization and social acceptance, because social regulations and their continuing demands distribution and development. This chapter considered different oral literature (including: Legend, Myth, Tales, Anecdotes, Epigram); dramatic literature (including: minstrelsy, pardekhani, threnody, chavoshi reading, women shows, ashiqha, poem reading and shahname reading). It goes through different independents (including: Poem, Riddle, puzzle, apothegm, typists, gvrngarhha, mementoes and graffito, writings on objects, oath, orison, curse and abusive) and children's literature (including: lullabies, coquetry and caress songs, playing song, proverb). As language is the main core for culture especially from the view point of

Worf and Saiper, it is also the main discussions of this chapter, which has a special importance in structuralism approach. They know language as the fundamental tools to understand human being behavior and their views about routine life and the way they analyze and describe it. Therefore, cultural anthropology acquires more knowledge through consideration of language in different communities, people thinking methods and their worldview and it tries to have a more suitable description and analysis. In another word, through analyzing of community language, we can acquire information about culture and thinking method of that society and its influence on language. In structuralism approach, culture is like language. Structuralism intensely takes affect from works of linguistic fields. Concentration of structuralism approach on culture depends on the recognition of analogic elements (signs and conceptions) and discovery of method, which organizes elements to send a message.

Written Literature

In accordance with anthropology definition, culture is the life style of a community, it is a combination of "far" as prefix, meaning in front and "hang" from Avesta tang root, means pulling and training. This definition is equal to Latina words means teaching and training. Sometimes it replaces with culture meaning civilization and it is a land, which has culture or cultural area.

Every society enjoys from special prototype for cultural generalities, which includes necessary organizations for human being like social, religious, political, economic, and materialized culture (tools, weapons and clothes). However, the reason for calling dictionaries and scientific proverbs book or scholars as culture is that these books and materials manifest the public culture of a nation; it is the common language, or special culture for scientific conventions and proverbs for some investigators of human being communities.

Books and written scripts for every era are symbol for that era culture. Culture as word used in ancient Persian poems: "you are a guide for every good and bad (Ferdowsi)"; (a cultural man does not put desire ship in this sea (Khaghani). Moreover, we witness for it between Islamic culture in Quran, which expresses original Islamic customs, and culture. Its best sample is Loqman advices to his son about "encouraging to goods and prohibition from bad" "avoiding from selfish behaviors", "encouraging for moderation and tranquility in society", "donations and endowment culture", "respect to parents", "culture to avoid from chaffing, animadversion and wrong names", "culture to avoid from man killing and bad actions", etc…

Visualization History

This is the oldest and the most important written works of ancient ages of Arzhang Mani. Mani was among those visualizers who could attract all audience's attention through image and miracle and he optimally used the specific value and very important of image and its role to send messages and having connection and influence on audiences.[1] Ali Masoudi, Yahya Dowlatshahi, and HosseinAli MoayedPardazi are famous painters of this type which later their method continued by some visualizers like Lili Taqipoor and Teymour Rashidi. Lili Taqipoor is the first Iranian visualizer woman who tends toward nature and she does not like the modern view.

During the half of the 20th century when it is the time for invasion of different information (because of quick growth for radio and television), pictures were not just description for news, however they induced thoughts and conceptions. Hereby the mental conception was a tangible reality and they used it in artistic works like a structural element. Then

---

1. MehrdadFar (2011), 26-28

the designer holding visual imagination took the responsibility to describe and elaborate on author text.[1]

Illustrations

Illustrations witness for this claim that whatever authors express through words, painters can visualize them in front of our eyes inside their pictures in compressed form. Although visualizers use visual codes not only to have relation with text but also they use them for bringing conception. Visualization is the oldest methods to express human and it is the most powerful system for non-verbal signs. Visualization means using visual signs in figure. Thinking process is impossible without imagination. Picture shapes human thought. In another word, illustration is a kind of painting produces in restriction of creator, in relation with text and observing special users. For that reason, it is natural that by a mother view (painter take influence and he reflects painting changes and revolutions naturally in visualizations. Although the history for miniature is the same for the history of visualization revolutions, it separated itself from painting gradually, after the entrance of printing industry to Iran.[2]

Human being always felt the need for studying and they try to write down and promote their emotions and thoughts.

By referring to internet bases for different television networks, we can understand the above-mentioned intentions. The introduction section of the channel 3, for example, includes the promotion of religious believes, and monotheistic view among youth and teenagers,

---

1. *Ibid*, 89-93
2. Afshar Mohajer (2011)

enhancement of information and their love and dependence to country. Moreover religion, history, culture and Iranian Islamic civilization in order to empower Islamic national identity based on revolution and reinforcement of avoiding from attractive and persuading appearances of western life among youth and teenagers and their security against western cultural aggression, enhancement of their knowledge about values of Islamic revolutions and holy defense expressed as its goals.[1]

Persian Prose

Persian prose since the mid of Naseredin Shah government chose a quick way toward simplicity, modernity movement started from the last decades of the 13th hijri century to literature, led to expanded transformations in appearance and content of prose. Authors like Molkom Khan, Akhoondzade, Mirza agha Khan Kermani and Zeinolabedine Maragheii simultaneous with the development of new thoughts emphasized on appearance simplicity and content usability. This are prose by providing new elegances like writing of memoir, writing of travelogue and writing of essays were a suitable bed for the formation of modern thought, which finally led to the emergence of constitutionalism literature.

Closeness of prose to conversational language and gradual replacement of poem with prose to express intention together with mental and cultural revolutions of that era, paved the way for authors including women writers to prose. Before the Naseri period, the samples

---

1. Abdollahi (2012), 92

remained form women prose are in limited form of religious thesis, although it might be that there have been other samples for women prose during history, but we do not have anything and the first experience of women relates in Naseri period. By following and making comparison between women writings, it becomes obvious that how women prose during less than few decades, changed from expression of emotions and feelings and individual issues toward reasoning, analyzing and description of social issues.

Rereading of culture and literature based on women attendance in texts and culture seems to be a kind of feministic critics in which women are object not scenario. The sovereignty of masculine culture over the Hindu-European ethnics has several thousand backgrounds. This sovereignty of this culture on literature and history is the reason why our literal and historical works are generally of masculine type, which describe and elaborate on men experiences. Traditionally, always three area of power in family and society, public and outside space and resources and literature as writer or audience belonged to men.[1]

Here are some reasons for the limitation of texts written by women:

1. In old community, complete separation of the public ground from private one was prevalent. Women belonged to the private section. She had to keep her closed and complete individual community, which had not any interruption with external world, no one could hear her

---

1. Milani (1992), 405

voice, she could not talk to anyone about her biography, and she shall preserve her bodily cover completely. Women belonged to a lonely and private world and their bodily or speaking manifestation just restricted to their family life cycle. For that reason, except some exceptional cases, the existence of a woman depended on her visibility or non-visibility and it defined through her silence and non-participation in society. Therefore, social values governing over women had consistency with their literal expression.[1]

2. Society of that time accepted the relation between woman and culture. Great poets and authors knew woman as the real nature and they defined man as the real wisdom and cultures. People did not respect women and they did not pay attention to them. In contrast to poem, prose was the ground to show wisdom and logic not imagination, therefore, women did not call for these fields.

3. Illiteracy women, poem composing did not need high literacy, however for prose speech it was necessary to be illiterate.

4. The reason for women tendency toward poem is that poem has been our oral and folklore culture. Songs, mothers' lullaby, complains, moans and mournful, happy poems all are a part of Iranian oral and speaking culture in which women created or preserved them. We shall not forget folklore stories and mothers and grandmothers narration; However most of these narrations did not

---

1. *Ibid*, 46

record and they have not written form. Whereupon, women have been story narrators and they did not belong to written culture.[1]

Investigation about the first prose experiences by women and making comparison with the next periods that is constitutionalism shows the movement and revolution for women prose from its first place, which took influence from conversational and private literature toward the secondary location and the public part for written literature.

It was because of the entrance of the new words like: democracy, parliament, law, homeland, freedom, which made prose as a device to express social and cultural issues. On the other hand, adventures frame memories and essay writing in newspapers, report prose became close to public culture and it was a suitable ground to express realities. Through consideration of written texts, we come to three frames: letter, adventures writing and social- critical thesis.

Letters manifest the conditions of people life and family disputes. Adventures writing are about customs of different ethnics in different cities and social-critical thesis talked about teaching, customs, and relations, which gave, right to men and compulsory for women. This view motivated women objection. Women authors in their book mention to bad behavior of men.

Summary

Chapter 5 especially considered the written culture. Written scripts and books for each era is a symbol for that era culture. For written culture or written literature, there are mentions to visualization, because visualization or

---

1. Grin & et. al (2004), 344

painting has been the first human being written works, which used it for concepts transferring. Most scientists believe that, image against written text and prose against poem has more depth influence over society culture. One of the oldest and the most important pictorial written texts of ancient era is Arzhang Mani. Mani was a visualizer who could attract audience's attention through image and miracle; he could optimally take advantage from special and important value of image and its role in order to send message and bring about relation and influence on audience. In the half of the 20th century when different information invaded because of the quick growth of radio and television and images were not descriptions for news, they induced thoughts and conceptions. Therefore, mental conception was a tangible reality and it used in artistic works like a structural element.

Persian prose and its history is another topic of this chapter. The entrance of words like, democracy, law, home country paved the way for the prose freedom to express social and cultural contents. On the other hand, adventures frame memories and essay writing in newspapers, report prose became close to public culture and it was a suitable ground to express realities and culture of every society.

Chapter 6

Past records and Consideration of the Previous Researches

History
Handwriting History

Ancient humans lived nomadically and probably they had the preliminary speaking. Artistic and stone works from that era holding elegance and artistic thought show that they did not use body language and imitation for their relation, they had speech (oral) relation. Before the invention of handwriting, people transferred his experiences orally. This called "chest to chest" relation. When he became speaker, there were different languages with the same root. Since handwriting invention, Iranian people used stone and mud, animal skin and leaf of trees for writing. During archeologic excavations in Oranvansa region, there were texts written on leather belonged to Parthians period. Abooabdollah Ebne Hamze Esfahani (born on 270 hijri) writes in his book that during his life, one old building ruined in Esfahan and they found book packaged in material Mongoose Plant skin called Tooz.[1]

---

1. Babolhavaeji (2002)

History of the Emergence of Printing in Iran

The first printing device established in Esfahan during Safavian period, which called Besme Khane and then changed to Matba^{c}e. It had Arabic and Persian letters and its establishment dates back to the first period of the 11th Hijri century. Another Printing house established in Esfahan at the same period dedicated to Armenians (About 1113 hijri), they used wood letters, and there they published their religious books. During these years, Ashoorian established a printing house to publish their religious books in Rezaeeye. In 1227 hijri when Fathali Shah was the king of Qajarian period, some Iranian people through the efforts of Abbas Mirza learned this technic in Europe and they brought the stone and lead printing device to Iran. The first lead printing house established in Tabriz and the first Persian printed book was "Fath Name" thesis written by Mirza Abolghaseme QaemMagham. During its early days for lead printing in Iran, molds like calico stamp prepared from hard wood and printed beside the lead letters to print images. The first pictorial lead printed book is Mokhtar Name. The industry of lead printing outmoded for a while, as people were not familiar with its working method. The first stone printing started up in Tabriz by Mirza Saleh Shirazi. Mirza Saleh who went to Europe by government to learn the new arts and he learned production of printing ink and preparing letters for printing house in London, brought a stone printing device when returning to Tabriz and started it on 1250 hijri. Stone printing house started in Tehran at the next 10 years, then Esfahan and other big cities established it, and it was the only printing method for more than 5o years. 8 years before the entrance of stone printing to Iran, people used lead printing but as it were expensive and a very hard job, people left it after the entrance of stone printing. At the end of Qajar period, again people used leadی printing. Stone printing books written with Nstaliq had pictures and gilding. Stone printing books had the same specifications like hand written books and they had different gilding, Tasheer (decorated margins have made with plants and animal pictures), Shamse, Arabesque designs, bergamot and half bergamot and inscription building, srlouh sazi, margins building, tableau building. Probably the first stone printed pictorial book was Leili & Majnoon of Maktabi Shirazi, which printed in Tabriz and Saadi Golestan published in 1286 hijri in Tehran and it was the highest quality stone printed book. By the emergence of modernity movements at the end of Qajar period and then constitutionalism revolution, newspapers and presses came to existence. The first Iranian newspaper called News Paper or Kaghaze Akhbar published by Mirza Saleh Shirazi in 1253 hijri and BRITISH museum holds two versions of it. News Paper handwriting was Nastaliq and it published by stone printing method in 82×4 cm. The leadی printing method was simple; they compressed paper over a page included ridged lead letters and sank in ink so letters went to paper. Newspapers letter writing was first with hand but then Linotype devices performed this work. At the next periods and especially during the second half of the 20th century had a very quick progress and even now, the most modern computer printing devices do this job. The first great step to the progress of printing technic was the invention of the transferrable letters invented by Youhan Gutenberg "gold maker with German genius" during 7931-8641 who called his first printing machine "rotation machine." This machine could print 70 to 100 papers in one hour and they stickink with hand. Printing devices and machines equipped more and rubber and Indian rubber machines used roller to distribute ink replaced for wood and rotational machines. Therefore, it facilitated printing on paper. Then, small printing machines called Minzo came to existence and horizontal machines replaced for vertical ones. Today, printing industry progresses momently together with communicational science for technique and speed progress. The daily progress of computer brings about astonishing transformation in this industry. Using computer for publishing has the name Desktop Publishing, because every text on display in front of operator eyes is like his private working table.

The Invention of Printing

In long times ago, book had monopoly for special people. One reason was the limited quantity of books because paper production and provision of script versions of book was very expensive and difficult and it was not cost effective for public people. In addition, special people enjoyed from the preliminary literacy. Book gathering was an entertainment for rich people and kings; they collected a great wealth by book gathering. Need of science lovers who were not rich made the increase for more books. Based on documents from past periods, printing date, relates in the 5 century before Christ that is about Achamedian period, when they used wood stamps to sign documents. This is the oldest printing type, called wood printing.

The History of Press in Iran

Press history in its general meaning in Iran, dates back to 1232 hijri when the first printed book emerged in Tabria or specifically 1253 hijri when Mirza Saleh newspaper published in Tehran. The first Iranian newspaper called Kaghaze Akhbar published since 1253 hijri until next years with long intervals. On 1267 hijri, Mirza Taqikhan published Vaqaye Etefaqiye and on 1277, they published 470 editions with the same name and format. Edition number 471 had not the word Vaqaye in its name and subsequently number 472 became famous with this name News Paper of government against IRAN. Mirza Hossein Khan Moshir o Dolleh when working as minister for Justice and War Ministries published Elmiye and Nezamiye News Papers, which were among the good newspapers of that period. On 1314 - 1324 Hijri, in addition to the previous newspapers, there published tens of weekly and monthly newspapers and the most famous ones were the two newspapers called Training and Polite. At the end of 1324 hijri, a total of 58 periodical newspapers and about 20 Persian newspaper and tens of night letters published in Iran and other countries respectively.[1]

---

1. Ansari Lari (1996)

When constitutionalism command issued, on Shaval 1324 Hijri, after this issuance, three new newspapers published and during these years, presses worked for social movements and they were mirror for thoughts and different ideas of people. During 1328 and 1329 hijri, the number of Tehran and provinces newspapers increased and the quantity of press publication talking about different parties was unexpectedly. At the last decade before the coup of 1920, presses had very unstable conditions. Based on what authors recorded, press date from 1836 to 1925, that is the starting point of Pahlavi Kingdom, there were more than 983 periodical presses 179 of them were the main and sub presses and more than 90 record letter published in Iran.

One month after the beginning of Mohammad Ali Shah period that is the early 1325 hijri, the Impressions ministry disbanded and the science and education ministry accepted some of its duties restricted to supervision for publishing houses, government newspaper, and patent issuance and press crimes affairs. At the same year two offices opened in this ministry to perform duties of education ministry. The specification of the year 1325 was unique in Iran Press History. During 73 years, there were about 91 periodical presses in Iran, but suddenly 99 presses came to press market, among them 64 press were for Tehran, 9 for Esfahan, 7 for Rasht, 6 for Tabriz, 4 for Hamedan, 2 for Lahijan, 2 for oromia, and 1 for Kermanshah, Shiraz and Mashhad.

The History of Publication Industry in Iran

Generally book publishing market is one hundred years old and it center is in capital city. This is the same for other countries and the capital city is the center for all publishers. (America is the exception, where Newborn is the center for all publishers). The first generation of Iran publishers, although started their jobs in Bazar and Timche Hajebodolle, Bazare Beinolharamein and Naser Khosro street, but by the development of Tehran city, they developed their book stores to Shah abad and Naderi (Jomhouri Eslami) street and then in front of Tehran university. One of the famous names for the first generation of Iran publishers are "Elmiha", established by Mirza Ali Akbar Khan Khansari who was a book seller in Khansar and after coming to Tehran, he established a book store in Timche Hajebodolleh. His son, Mirza Mohammad Esmaeel, first with his father and then independently opened a store in Naseriye Street (Naser Khosro) for the next years and thought about printing and publishing. Then he heard that in Mashhad, Russians want to sell a printing house. Mirza Mohammad Esmaeel, (now he was Haji) went to Mashhad, bought one stone printing machine together with it's accessories and brought them to Tehran. He started book printing and together with his five sons, established bookstores in front of Tehran University under the scientific name of "Javidan Publishing".

Late Nasrollah Saboohi founder of "Book Selling and Central Publishing" was also in Naser Khosro Street. (After the establishment of Publishers and Booksellers Unity in

Tehran, was one of the first chairpersons of this unity).
Mohammad Ramezani held Kalale Khavar publishing.
(Which was first located in Lalezar and then transferred to
Shah Abad near to Sayyed Hesahm alley and then to
Ekbatan Street). He was also among the pioneers of the first
publisher generation in Iran. He published the first special
and independent quarterly press about book called book
quarterly in 64 pages on Farvardin, 1943. Of this,
quarterly just four versions published and then stopped
publishing. Then he published a weekly pamphlet called
"Afsane" in 8 to 16 pages, which introduced the world
literature, and some of the Persian works. "Afsane"
pamphlets show the important part of Iran cultural
activities during 1921 to 1931.

The first generation of Iranian publisher before 1921,
10 publishing institutions and between 1900 to 1931,
totally established 16 publishing institutions. During
decades 30, 40 and 50, gradually the second generation of
Iranian publishers came to existence. This generation,
holds the specification of "acculturation." These groups
know foreign languages, some of them are author,
translator and literal critics and they plan to inject new
blood to book publishing industry. Among the second
generation of Iranian publishers, this job does not transfer
from father to his son and their approach toward book
publishing is not aninherited job. Publishing institutes
like: Nil, Zaman, Agah, Morvarid, Kharazmi, Rowzan,
Sepehr, Toos, Donya, Bamdad, Dehkhoda and others
founded by those who did not performed this job by
heritage. Acculturation and having information about the
modern literature, was their motivation to establish these
institutes, some of which came with shareholders and

their stocks (Like: Kharazmi publishers institute or publishers company). The first generation had tendency toward persian classic literature and religious texts, however, the second generation was the representative for the persian and the world modern literature. The most share for publishing modern persian and non-persian works owes to the second generation of book publishers in Iran. all works by Sartr, Kamo and generally committed literature and existentiality works, modern dramas and Hemingway, Falkner and Stein bach and new European and American literature reached to the eager readers by these publishers in decades 30, 40 and 50.

However, the third generation of persian publishers continued their job to the foreign countries. The same conditions and motivations together with situations and social changes in Iran attracted some groups to book publishing field. Iranian publishers outside the country are the continuation for the third generation. approximately the same factors and motivations which bring about the third generation inside the Iran, emerged the persian publishing industry in abroad which generally summarizes in two main parts: Utopians (to progress political, national, religious and cultural goals) and economic factor(as a new field to earn money for an emigrant).

Summary

This chapter goes through consideration of the past records and researches. First, we expressed handwriting history, artistic works and stone devices holding artistic elegance and thought tell us that the ancient people did not use body language or imitation for connection, they had oral relation. The history for printing industry in Iran dates back to the first printing device during Safavie period in Esfahan.

During ancient times book and knowledge was in monopoly of the special people. Book gathering was an entertainment for rich people and kings, through which they saved a great wealth. The need of knowledge lovers who were not rich led to the increase of scripts quantities. One reason was the restriction for books, because paper production and the provision of handwritten scripts were very difficult and expensive and it was not economically profitable for public people.

Press history in its general meaning in Iran, dates back to 1232 hijri when the first printed book emerged in Tabriz or specifically 1253 hijri when Mirza Saleh News Paper published in Tehran. Printing industry goes gradually together with communication sciences and progresses daily and computer made astonishing transformation for this industry. Using computer for publishing is famous as desktop publishing; therefore, every text on display in front of operator eyes is like his personal table.

This chapter also considered the history for publishing industry in Iran. Publishing industry is a 100 years old art and its center is in Tehran. Before 1921, there were just 10 publishing institution, which faced with a daily growth after decade 40 and 50.

Chapter 7

Comparative Studies of Culture

Introduction

It goes without saying that managers, staff, client, suppliers and even capital holders do not cooperate in an environment free from values and regulations. Their working method, connection, and cooperation with each other surely directly or indirectly takes influence of believes values and in way that is more limited it is under the influence of social and organizational culture and even guides with it. Special and dedicated values, believes, habits, attitudes and systems which are unique and general for an organization and society, shape their culture. As Wilson (1992) said, culture gradually becomes a treat for all organization diseases.

Cultural differences between communities, countries and nations, have a major role in designing, regulation, and implementation of strategic designs and thinking and attitudes of strategic managers. In an era when every strategic management activity has relation with other communities, nations and governments, for those strategic global managers, regulation, and execution of strategy in new environment will be more difficult and complex. Some of the third countries companies, which experience global activities or those who experienced them before, believe that most of the global problems root in cultural, economic, political, training, and teaching, environment differences and the different methods to use production resources.

The subject of culture, for that reason, holds specific importance in strategic management and by the emergence of global business and similar events, this topic becomes more important for success, as national culture and sub cultures also have depth influence on working and duties of national and local governments.

In his famous and important researches, Hafstede, wrote his research results in a book called culture and organization, which includes very important points including cultural differences. He could successfully express these differences and their effects on works and business especially in global business and he helped a lot for the resolution of unknown cultural issues.

He believes that the major cultural differences among nations root in their attitudes, values and believes. His investigation can help scientists, authors and researchers to regulate and draw their own cultural differences against other cultures.

Probably the most important cultural differences among nations have the highest grade of avoiding from danger in making decisions. His result is that the more differences among community people, there is more dangers for making decisions. If power distance between community people, for instance, is high for different levels, it will be an obstacle between nations and the less this distance is, it facilitate cooperation, because in first part, cooperation with these nations or groups just limits to powerful people.

It seems that global business and transactions relate more with interests and using opportunities and avoiding from threats and all of them originate in cultural factors, which have role in success or failure. Powerful people are more or less aware about it and here we can mention to competition of Japan with other East Asia countries.

If we really accept that cultural subjects are effective in selection of strategy and its implementation and they have close relations with global transactions, therefore, it is necessary to have a more depth look to it.

Culture, Views and Attitudes

Attraction and attention to organizational culture started in 1980 decade through works of Allen & Kraft, 1982 and Deal & Kennedy, 1982, and the more important one works of Peters & Waterman, 1982. Although university men considered it many years ago, as Al Air & Fiersirto (1984) and Albero (1997) did show, before 1982 and Piterz theory, many theories developed about culture. Turner theory, 1971 and Blake & Mouton, 1969 are the examples. On 1986, Turner connected the topic of decreasing products quality standard on 1980 in America and Japanese economic success to culture or what he says, "mad culture." His suggestion was that culture brought about new method to recognize and paying attention to organization and many authors recognized culture as the secret of Japanese economic success in decade 70 and 80. Among them Bowels 1989 believes that among western and developed economic countries, culture has little role or there is not at all and this issue potentially produced a force which created believes systems and fictions inside the organizations. It gave excellent opportunities to promote and improve organization and society through culture relations. Deal and Kennedy elegantly used culture topic. They know culture as the first motivation for organization movement instead of organizational structure, strategy and policy.

On the other hand, Silverman, 1970 believed that organization is a miniature shape of society, for that reason, we expect it to show signs and witnesses of its own society specifications. Although culture is not something, which shapes suddenly and automatically from wishes and desires, however, Alair and Firsirto 1984 believed that culture is the product of the influence of different factors and elements shape during times. Moreover, it includes society values, specifications, history and the past time of organization, past leaders of organization and other factors like technology, industry type and educational level and other authors delivered lists similar to the above factors. Drenna, 1992, for instance, expressed organization expectations topic as the elements shaping culture, but it is easy to know this as the organization reaction about values. As Kaming & Huse, 1982: 421, expressed, organization values shape key and the main elements of organizational culture. Of course, it is possible to recognize elements, which shape culture and their reflection, they believed that there is a real difficulty to recognize and understand the meaning of culture for an organization.

Brown, 1995, estimated that there are hundreds of different definitions for culture; some of them are as follows:

- Culture is common thinking and view, common emotion and action in a social group.
- Culture is mental programming.
- Culture is an expanded word, which shapes the prototype for thinking, feeling, and action performing for each person in organization and society.
- Culture is common phenomenon and group life accepted and used by group of people.
- Culture for factory is thinking and action method, which changed to a habit and originates from tradition and members more or less accepted it and the new persons should learn it.
- Culture is design and prototype related in common believes and expectations between members of organization. These believes and expectations shape behaviors of organization persons and groups.
- Culture is the quality to receive organizational specialties and professions including the process of abnormal quality, which distinguish it from others in one industry.
- Common believes and understanding of senior managers of an organization about methods to monitor organization and personnel.
- It might be that the most prevalent definition with expanded usage is definitions delivered by Eldrige &

Crombi, 1974 or Geert Hofstede, 1989-1991 which are as follows:

Culture is the shape and combination of forms, standards, values, believes and ways people and organization use it specifically or specifications or style and method, which people and groups use them to perform integration and combination.

Culture says about the way to act in organization in different situations. Culture affects everybody from senior managers to high-class officials and the simple workers.

Their actions evaluate and judges by themselves and others based on the behavioral prototype. Culture always talks about a special method of manners, which is legal, and logic and simultaneously describes other forms. This view point of Turner on 1971 supported by others, he observed that cultural systems hold elements of does and do not's, doing and not doing which shape behavior form and permit special actions by people and people judge based on these acceptable or non-acceptable behaviors.

On the other hand, Hafstede defines culture as a common thinking and view, common feeling and action in one social group. He believes that as emotion, action, and attitude and thinking method of the members of a society (village, city, province, organization or country) is different, therefore, their culture is different. These groups can have common thoughts, feelings, and actions, which shape a society and in other place, Hafstede expresses culture as mental programming. Every person has a mental paradigm for his behaviors, which makes decision based on them, and he calls common paradigm as culture. Other scientists, suggested different dimensions of culture, which leads to behavior. Martine and others 1983, express the role of organization history to shape culture and organization expectations from personnel. They expressed seven preliminary type of general organization history, which can deliver a fundamental answer for specific manner of personnel which includes:

1. Do personnel can ignore rules or not?

2. Is the senior chairperson of an organization is a human?

3. Do the simple personnel can promote to the highest place?

4. Do they deport me?

5. Does organization help me, if I want to do an action?

6. How is the reaction of bosses to mistakes?

7. How organizations face with obstacles and issues?

During historical investigations, there are many attentions to the role of ceremonies, customs, religions, and the method to empower actions.

Trice & Beyer, 1984 recognized them including the following issues:

• Rites of passage, designing to facilitate changing signs in high posts and people role to pass events like teaching and training and survival and stability programs.

• Rites of questioning which permits people asking questions about the existing and status-quo, including by consultants outside the organization?

• Rites of renewal, which permits to revise the current situation by contribution and innovation, this issue includes strategy development, bringing about new attitude and view and revision designing programs for occupations.

Another important issue expressed in literature and written texts is the role of heroes. Peters & Eterman, 1982 expressed the importance of company heroes to bring about opportunity for having higher posts for their relations. Deal & Kennedy, 1982 know heroes as the greatest motivations for companies. Most part of the company's success assigns to the actions and personalities of people like Andrew Carnegie, Henry Ford and Alfred Sloan.

Nowadays, heroes like Bill Gates in Microsoft, Steve Jobs in Apple and Jack Welch in General Electric and many others in different countries (what we mean by heroes in this discussion is the existence of genius people in companies which paved the way for popularity and the success of company).

On 1995, Brown delivered a long list for cultural factors. This list helps us to understand and recognize the influence of cultural factors on people and groups behaviors.

As Brown said the introducing of a long list about cultural factors not only is effective to know culture, but also it can divert us, because it is difficult to recognize that which factor is more important or less important to change culture. Authors, of course, tried a lot to categorize and introduce the major factors, which we will introduce them completely in the next chapter. Hafstede, 1990, as we will see in next chapter, delivered a four categorized cultural model, in hierarchical way under the title of cultural onion:

1. Signs stay in higher place
2. Heroes are in the next place
3. The next place devotes to customs and values stay at the center of onion.

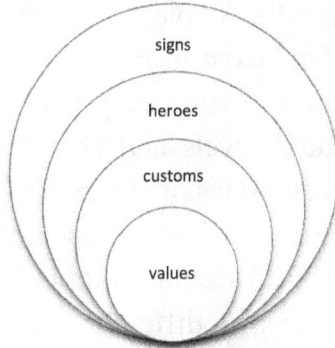

Schein, 1985, delivered a three layers model based on the first hypothesis like believing in God in the most depth layer, believes values and attitudes in middle level and artificial works in the first level and the external level.

On the other hand, Kiuming & Huse, 1989 compiled and delivered an integrated model including four major elements based on analysis for different definitions of culture.

1. Basic assumptions, includes cultural information, which exist unconsciously in the most depth level. The provided hypothesizes talks about solutions for organizational issues. They are about introducing those non-debatable and annoying hypothesizes about environment, labor force and their activities and human relations.

2. Values are the second and highest information and recognition about value. They tell us about what shall be and what shall not be in organization. Values announce people of an organization about important and non-important issues.

3. Norms exist exactly under the cultural information, norms, and references to guide and lead activities of

organization members. This section includes non-written rules and regulations for people behaviors.

4. Artificial affairs exist in the highest level of cultural information, which are completely visible and expressing against other cultural levels and shaping and recognized factors and elements. This includes visible behaviors of members, systems, methods, techniques, rules and regulations and physical sections of organization.

Although delivering different cultural levels by different authors can be effective to recognize culture, but as Brown, 1995, said we shall pay attention to this point that organizational practical culture is not always the same as models and it has sometimes, fundamental differences with models caused from many other factors, which are not in the said models.

As different scientists tried to introduce organizational culture and its levels and layers, there were other efforts to categorize and introduce different cultures. Deal & Kendel, 1982 recognized and introduced four types of culture: Togay McCo, introduced culture as person originality and the amount, which he accepts, dangers. Work Hard & Poly Hard, defines culture through accepting low level of danger and quick reflection of the recognized function. McDonald is an example for the best organizational culture by accepting high danger and longtime reflection. Airlines and cultural process introduced as the organizations accepting the less danger and gradual reflection like insurance companies.

Quinn & McGrath, 1995, recognized and introduced four types of culture. Bazar delivered by personnel through logical decisions and tendency toward goals. Specific affairs of temporary organizations (Adhocracy) which guided toward danger and spiritual leaders and rejected and guided organizations by values; like Apple and Microsoft during their first years of activity. Family and clan, which recognized through contribution, cooperation, and paying attention to others problems, like volunteer organizations. Hierarchy: This type of organization introduced by hierarchies, legal authorities, stable values, they avoid from danger, like Ministries and governmental organizations.

It might be that the best recognized models for culture and the oldest one developed and expanded on 1986 by Hendi. He observed and introduced four types of culture; power and authority, personal and individual, roles, and duty. He related each factor especially to organizational structure.

Aauthority culture, he observed and recognized this power among small organizations like financial, commercial and home appliances. This culture has network structure and it relates to two or more senior characters who work at the center of company.

Individual culture, he rarely talked about this case. Person wishes exist at the center of this culture. This type of culture relates in minimum structure and it goes to relate personnel who want to work with each other. Personal culture, therefore, can be like the complex of individual stars in sky.

Roles culture, this type of culture dedicates to mechanical, bureaucratic, robotic, and non-tangible structures and small jobs. This type of culture mostly pays attention to methods, roles, power hierarchies, security, and anticipation of events and operations. This culture brings about a situation in organization, which the individual sinks in his duties and refers any anticipation to other level based on hierarchy.

Task culture, on the other hand, this type of culture just tends toward job and duty. The only responsibility is performing job (duty) not job quality. This type of culture is suitable for those organic organizations, which are tangible and encourage group working. Duty culture, brings about a situation in which the quick reflection and reaction, convergence and creativity is very important, even more important than sticking to methods and special rules. Here powers, authorities, and duty are less important than personal help to perform duties.

Hendi believed that these two last cultures that is the culture of role and duty, which mostly exist in western cultures, relates in BURN & STALKER, 1961, under the title of continuous structure with mechanical structures in one hand and organic structures on the other hand.

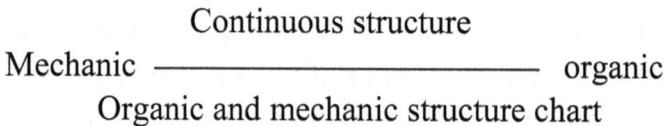

Continuous structure

Mechanic ———————————— organic

Organic and mechanic structure chart

Here we see that under the influence of this model, Hindi tries to structuralize the parallel shapes, it is in relation with the above continuous structure, in which roles culture stays in one direction, the other direction is for duty culture, and the end is for organic section.

This type of categorization surely has consistency with five western approaches for organizational theories discussion. Adaptation of Japanese organizations with this framework is very difficult, because their culture has elements of the two parts of the above model. Japanese have hard and intense jobs structures especially for low ranks. Hierarchies and variety have great influence on them. They are simultaneously very motivated, creative especially for problem solving. They are very interested toward group working and handling internal affairs with complete freedom (self-tendency).

Probably the most critics for this type of categorization and ranking for culture is that they do not devote high value to national culture and its influence on organizational cultures. National culture surely governs over organizational culture and the influence of national culture over organizational cultures in different countries is different.

During the past decade, there were very intense conditions about organizational theories and management theories for one culture or a society,[1] especially, between western and Asian cultures and it uses for other organizations (Ho, 1976).

According to sulivan & nonaka (1986), all models of organizational culture are producing and publishing by developed countries, especially North America and of course this is a very serious criticism.

Most of the prevalent and comprehensive works for cultural differences between nations is a work performed by "Hafstede," between 1980-1990 and we will consider it in the next chapter and here we mention to its

---

1. Rosenaweig (1994)

summary. He suggested that it is possible to categorize national culture based on their similarities:

1. The superiority of individuals or the group origins for each country.

2. Gap between power and authority accepted in each country.

3. The amount and degree of risk taking or risk avoiding.

Based on these cultural dimensions, "Hafstede" could categorize industrial countries in four groups:

1. Scandinavian countries including; Denmark, Sweden and Norway; this culture is based on group originality, and concentration.

2. West Germany (during this research, Germany was not a one and only country), Swiss, Austria, these cultures devote high value to profitability. It is a machine lubricated precisely and they try a lot to decrease dangers.

3. Britain, Canada, North America, News land, Australia and Netherland; these countries stay between part 1 and 2. However, these values shape the individual originality in society.

4. Japan, France, Belgium, Spain, and Italy, they love bureaucracy. Their structure is pyramidal and there is a great distance between power and authority among seniors and ordinary people.

According Wilson 1992, similarity of cultural factors of "Hafstede" and four organizational forms expressed by Hendi have relation with each other. It is possible to put Scandinavian culture in category of Hendi for duty culture, and we put West Germany in Roles Cultures. However, the next two groups that are Britain and Japan do not easily stay in Hendi category. Britain and America stay in one group. Anyway, it is better to talk about details not generalities. Here we categorize culture and its debates based on viewpoints of investigators and authors in following four ranks:

First, based on Dale & Kenedi idea, it is better to shape behaviors through contribution in values, believes and the basic hypothesis for organization operations instead of bringing direct or indirect relation between people behavior and internal or external reflections. How to divide rewards and privileges, for instance, or sessions manners and even the way people wear clothes.

Second, if organization has its own personality, identity, and culture, these cases belong to those who work in higher posts.

Third, as Sathe, 1983, believes culture is a phenomenon, which guides organization members and operation, without needing to structuralize or descriptive teaching and details or needing to hold long time and exhausting sessions to solve a special issue. Even he can decrease misunderstanding between offices and sections and duties. He can bring about a general understanding and intentions to lead all of them toward one direction. However, here we shall pay attention that, this will execute when organization has a powerful culture, when members of organization never doubt about believes, values legitimacy and culture suitability of an organization.

Fourth, as Barratte, 1990, believes values, believes and viewpoints are learnable phenomenon and we can guide them or even change them, managers especially can lead them skillfully. Oreily, 1989, also believes that culture is guidable and changeable. It is possible to select, guide, and regulate culture based on behavior, attitude and views.

Changing Organizational Culture

There is no doubt about changing of organizational culture or its change in future; organizational culture is not a stable phenomenon. Because as factors and environment variables and internal variable of organization change, therefore, organizational culture will change too. However, if culture blocks and closes by believe, values and norms of every person, it is like a building, which its changing is, very difficult and changing this culture is very slow, unless we expect for a major and important shock to organization.[1] This is not problematic for organization, it make the change of other factor equally and slowly. Debates about superior culture say that a successful culture establishes based on suitable values and hypothesis about organizational environment and operations. Moreover, as Hendi, 1986 and Aliyer & Fiersto, 1984, believe, in order to perform effective and useful operations, they shall be proportion with organizational structure and they shall integrate with them. For that reason, organization environment is quickly changing and it can change structure. Conditions and situations show that when an organization leaves the line, that is when organization environment, structure or operation change quickly.

As Hendi believes, based on experiences, a powerful culture makes a powerful organization without paying attention to the type of culture. However, not all cultures are suitable for all people and intentions. Cultures recognized and found during long years by groups influencing on

---

1. Brown (1995)

organization. What has been suitable in a special period is not eternal and durable even if it is very powerful.

Felin, 1993, based on the philosophy for tendency toward bazar, explains that this situation happened for all governmental organization in England and similar situations happened in private sections (Brown, 1995). For that reason, and because of several reasons, organization can come to this conclusion that the existing culture is not a suitable one and even it can recognize this thought and decision to keep competition power. For this situation, all organizations decide to change the existing culture.

A similar research by the industrial community on 1997 performed for 4000 organizations. It shows that 90 percent of them are changing their cultures or they finished it. This research did show that cultural changes performed by using different models and methods including; strategic plans, teaching, structure renovation for promotion and establishment of working groups and changing the evaluation systems.

Dabson believes that if an organization decides to change its culture, it shall change believes and values and attitudes of its personnel. Based on operations that these companies performed to change culture, he introduced the following fourth step to change culture:

First Step: changing the employment and selection policies and to remove surplus items, so you can change labor force framework and therefore, personnel promotion performs based on believes and values which organization tends to promote them and employees manifest and provide them.

Second Step: organization labor force renews in order to become sure that managers and employees with suitable character and behavior occupy higher jobs.

Third Step: it is effective transfer for new values, which performs through different methods and by using different models like one to one interview, group justification, quality circles, internal newspaper, and advertisements. Senior managers shall manifest new values and believes. This will be very important and effective for change success.

Fourth Step: this is changing systems, methods, and policies for human resources especially those, which relate in rewards, evaluations, and followings.

Cumming & Huse, 1989, p. 428-30, recognized some steps which are the cause for success in culture changing. Their approach is strategic. They introduced the followings:

1. One Clear Strategic. Attitude that is effective cultural change in organization through clear and new strategy for organization and it continues by sharing and contribution of values and behaviors. This new attitude, provides the new intention and direction for cultures.

2. Commitment of the Senior Management. here the cultural changes shall guide and lead by senior managements. Senior managers and official managers shall powerfully commit and obligate themselves for new believe and values, they shall bring about a continuous pressure for change.

3. Symbolic Leadership. executive and senior managers shall transfer new culture to others through their personal practical actions, they shall be number one for their commitment. Their behavior shall symbolically manifest new values and behaviors for organization.

4. Support for Organizational Changes. cultural changes shall always perform together with structural modification and changes, human resources systems, information and control systems and management models. These organizational forms help to the guide and justification of organization members' behavior toward new culture.

5. Organization Members. This is one of the most effective tools to change organizational culture. People select based on new culture and their skills, they shall know exactly the required behavior, and attitudes. The employment contract with official employees, who cannot adapt themselves with new methods, shall terminate. Like early retirement and redemption, for instance, and similar cases, which are very important for sensitive and key Posts?

Culture and Strategic Management
Culture

For most times and especially for developing countries, plans and projects for economic, technologic, medical, biology, urban affairs are just technical and specialty projects and most of these projects faced with delay and budget shortage and rarely they were successful. One of the main reasons for this issue is ignoring differences between plans executers like thinking method, attitude, emotion, and comprehension. Especially regional projects and here we shall confess that recognition of these differences for plans and projects success has importance like specialty, technic and financial topics.

This chapter goal, which takes effect from book named; Culture and Organization by "Guiret Hafstede", can provide strategic managers with a very useful guide, and a reference for investigators and those who like cultural affairs and it was a very pity if strategic managers and readers could not use it.

Culture as Mental Programming

There is no doubt that every man and woman holds a framework for thinking, emotion, and action, which makes all decisions, based on them.

As much as differences exist between people, their mental framework is different too; of course, there are common factors among these varieties, which manifest mental structure of people for understanding and recognizing phenomenon and their differences. Most of these shape during childhood periods, because, child is ready to learn and imitate, he/she systemizes his works based on these imitations and simultaneously he/she shall not learn and feel a lot of things, unless he learns their basics, roots and reasons previously. of course, it is clear that during his first years of life, preventing himself from learning is more difficult than learning, something that makes everything difficult for parents.

Culture Definition

Managers normally perform works by others and this is prevalent all over the world. For this goal, manager shall know the ways and methods to do this and he shall recognize the best people for his goal. By recognizing people, we mean having information about their past records, education, their weak and power points and other specifications, to be able to anticipate their actions. Among their specifications, the most important part is their past records, which shape special culture for them, and it discovers their intangible and invisible behaviors.

Culture definition here is a series of mental programs, which distinguishes them from other people or societies. Members of groups or other communities can be members of other cities, societies, nations, regions and unities or woman against men, old against young, type of job, organization or even family.

On the other hand, Hafstede defines culture as common thinking and view, common feeling and action in one social group. He believes that, because group attitude, action, and emotion (like: village, city and province, country) can be different with other groups, therefore, their culture is different too; in addition, they can have commons in thinking, emotion, and action. Hafstede says that, these commons shape their group culture, for that reason, citizens of one city is different with the other city, however, those parts that are common for all cities, shape province culture, and culture of a province can be different with the other city. Something accepted by all provinces, shape their national culture, global culture, women and ethnic culture, and they do not have differences for national culture. All people live in one political-geographical land called country have many emotional, thinking and action commons which shape national culture.

On the other hand, culture is a learnable and acquiring phenomenon not a heritage, genetic one and it always transfers from social environment to people. On the other hand, culture distinguishes from instinct which is one hundred percent heritage and from people personality which is mental and heritage, although, sociologists and social sciences scholars have discussions for them.

Human Nature

Plato believed that when human born, he knows everything, human soul lived in other world before coming to human body, and it might be that he mentions to nature. Holy Quran says; that specific creation which we gave to human being.

Human characteristics expressed in humanitarian sciences, are nature. God has given those characteristics to human being. We use it for human being, nature can instinct in animal and it is inborn. It comes from human nature. Human being knows what he can knows, that is, every human being has a series of natures, and he knows them. Philosophers believe that the only way to values human knowledge and his philosophical thinking is accepting nature of the main basics of thinking theory.

They reject nature, they say, human mind does not need a series of fixed principles needed for wisdom. If as holy Quran says, we devote series of specifications from the first creation, this is nature, or inborn is specifications from the root of human creation.

Ebne Asir definesnature: it is the beginning and invention, it is the preliminary creation and it is a non-imitated creation.

Inborn is a philosophical debate about human being, God stays in one pole and on the other pole there is human being. Therefore, creation is a gradual issue, God created human being with his own specification; he gave man talent to grow his divine characters.

The basis of creation is right; every creation has his rights and duties. The cause of creation is using God grace by all creations and man shall use all gifts of God.

Inborn like nature and instinct is genetic, it is part of human nature and it is more conscious than instinct, we use instinct for animal, it is a semi-conscious manner and it relates in material subjects of animal.

One of the unknowns about human being as the most unknown creature is his inborn, which shapes by following sections:

1. for recognition, understanding, receiving
2. Needs and tendencies which divides in two parts:
   a) Bodily natural requirements
   b) Spiritual natural needs
3. For emotion, it includes searching for truth, tendency toward goodness and virtue, beauty, creativity, love and worship.

The existence of searching for justice, science, perfection, God and art all relates to nature. Because one of the reason that it relates in nature, is its continuity during history and they will not disappear because they always and forever live with human being.

If a need or requirement is not in human nature, it will forget gradually because of environmental, internal revolutions and life changes and it replaces with other subjects. Of course, we shall pay attention that because needs and intentions are different, the decrease of life affair leads to its replacement with other affairs, or paying attention to one or more wishes is necessary it influences other natural wishes and blocks their growth. Because natural specifications like acquiring ones need suitable conditions for their growth and flourishing, and if educational, training and social environments do not bring about suitable conditions for growth and development of a natural behavior, that specification disappears completely. In addition, it might be that because of wrong teachings or non-suitable tries to destroy his natural desire.

In brief, most of human behavior results from his nature, therefore it is a very powerful tool to guide and anticipate actions and reactions.

For that reason, we say that God has given nature to human being; it exists from his born to his death time. It exists among all human beings from different group, nation, ethnic, or tribe and it shapes physical and psychological activities, like fear, hunger, anger, love, happiness, sorrow, and social needs, which exist for all human beings. These people feel and understand, they afraid and become happy but its amount recognizes by culture. These instinct do not restrict to human being, animals have them too.

Personality

People personality is a series of mental and wisdom programs, which other people are partner with them, these results from heritage behaviors, which come by genetic, and part of it comes from living, working, and social environment.

This is definition of personality by psychology: it is a series of mental and bodily specifications and characters, whereupon by personality we meant a unity of outward factors and specifications and final motivations.

Permanent and stable specifications are people personality, if she is always smiling but sometimes we look her with bad tempered, her character is smiling, and she is not a bad tempered person. Two persons do not have similar personality. These personal specifications distinguish people from each other. Famous English psychologist, believes that it is rarely to find two person among one milliard people who have similar genes, in addition, during his life, a person learns from his family, school, society and experiences a lot, all of which form his personality and he has reasons for himself. Islamic scholars expressed interesting issues about personality. Human being is like a white slab when he comes to this world, which is ready to attract role and shape. Two important principles are effective for personality shaping: 1) existence of talent; 2) his dependence to environment. They say:

• Roles he accepted by his talent and from environment are not changeable.

• The growth of talent and changing potential to de facto, demands complete recognition of people talents.

• Through recognition of human talents, we can choose a suitable role for him.

• Human being role is conscious and free. Human being can freely select his future by his wisdom and will force.

Most scientists believe that personality shaping elements are different from genetic issues, and they mention to the role of other factors like; healthy personality, holding average intelligence, self-esteem, memory, trust, responsibility, power for making decision, innovation and thinking, anger controlling, mental concentration, appearance and health, punctuality, discipline and paying precise attention to job, speaking method, connection and communication methods.

Cultural behaviors are always of inherited type, because past professors and philosophers could not explain or justify outstanding differences of cultural paradigms between people and communities in another way. They understood and recognized effects and results of learning from past generations and they knew teaching these effects to their next generations. They expressed heritage role exaggeratedly in pseudo theories for races, like holocaust by Nazism during the second world war or racism and ethnic battles and fights justified through non-written and not found debates about cultural superiority and minority.

One of these hot cultural debates is about 1960 decades in America, whether black skins are less intelligent than white skins or not. This issue followed on decade 70 and after many researches about racism superiority, it became clear that people do not pay attention to this subject. It has not been popular and even intelligence and talent ranking for Asians who live in America was higher than white skins talent. Anyway, if it is not impossible, it is very difficult to perform any test without using culture for it, if it is possible, they just tested capabilities, and it is just reflection of abilities not differences or social opportunities. It is of no doubt that black skins in America had less opportunities than white skins had in this country.

Cultural Relativism

Among experiences acquired by cultural investigators, they found human group different in thinking, emotion, and action, but there was not a certain scientific criterion to measure these differences, which show the superior or minor group. Investigation about these cultural differences between different groups named "cultural relativism."

Claude Levi Strauss one of the famous French anthropologists believes that: "cultural relativism means that there is not a precise and certain index for judging about its difference with other culture. Therefore, it cannot say which one is superior and which one is minor, but culture shall be able to judge about his cultural activities, because its people are witness and actor for its role."

By culture relativism, it is not possible to understand that it has not form and criterion for itself or for society, its most attention is when you want to encounter with other communities or people culture. For that reason, everyone who is going to make comparison between his and others culture, shall think a lot.

Symbols, Heroes, Rituals and Values

Cultural differences show themselves through different methods. Among different methods and factors, four factors that are symbols, signs, heroes, rituals, and values can provide us with a general or precise and clear-cut meaning. The following figure shows these four factors like onion layers. It expresses the situation for each factor based on its depth. Symbols delivered by managers and officials stay in surface layer and values which have less changes stay in bottom, the other two factors are between the two above said factors.

```
        signs
       heroes
      customs
       values
```

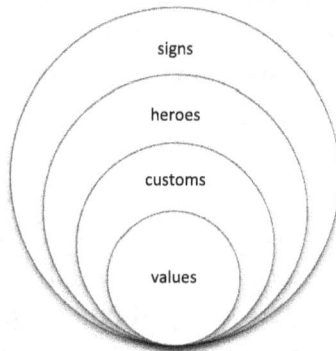

Cultural Onion

Symbols include words, pictures, forms, checklists and like them, every symbol has different meaning and usage, just people of the same community and culture know them. Slang words and idioms are in this group, which are special for each community and country. Face and head makeup, letters signs are also here. New signs are easily expandable, old signs easily delete, and even it is possible to use signs of other culture in another one. Therefore, for the above chart (cultural onion) signs are in the first (external) layer, which are easily separable.

On the other hand, there are people who are alive or died and their characters belong to their society, they are very respectful and lovely and people use them as paradigm. Like Imam Ali (peace be upon him) who is on the top of all world heroes, his name now is a value, is a respect and greatness or Pooriaye Vali who is in lower rank.

For third layer of cultural onion, we have rituals and ceremonies shaped during centuries in society and we observe them at present. It is a group activity meaning achieving to special goals in far and near past, but they are a specific and necessary event for itself. Like religious and national ceremonies or special, social or historical events.

The root and main cultural factor is values, which shapes the center for all cultural factors and elements for every society. When the past three symbols, heroes, and rituals are easily visible by foreign people, but its implementation meaning is not visible by people of other culture. Values are expanded and intense tendency of community toward the priority of one subject to the other one and it one hundred percent can be positive or negative about that special subject. Please pay attention to the following cases:

1. Beauty against ugliness
2. Goodness against badness
3. Clean against dirty
4. Natural against unnatural
5. Normal/abnormal
6. Logical/illogical
7. Reasonable/ unreasonable

Values are among all issues and knowledge, which children learn during their first process of life unconsciously.

Psychologists believe that children until 10 years old learn these preliminary culture values by themselves, and after that, it is very difficult to change these values. Because they became familiar with them during their first years of life and they have depth root inside them.

Whereupon we cannot discuss about them, and a foreign viewer cannot observe them directly. They are just understandable by their actions and behaviors in different conditions and situations. Meanwhile implementation of a systematic investigation for understanding of values for people actions and behaviors is very difficult and vague.

Up to now, many questionnaire researches implemented for the superiority and people selection and its different factors and solutions. It is not possible to express answers word for word, because people do not act as they say in questionnaire. Questionnaire always can provide usable and important information, because different people give different answers and categorization and totalizing of these answers can be usable. One group, for example, prefer less working hours and more salary, the other group give opposite answer and here it is possible to distinguish cultural and views differences.

It is important to bring difference between people claims and wishes and what they do in reality. Questions about wishes relate to the whole community, their answers are like; good/bad, correct/wrong, agree/disagree. Generally, every person is agreeing with good actions, and he disagrees with sin, but in reality, everything is different. However, what distinguishes between wishes and reality relates in reference and samples nature.

Forms are true for wishes, they relate to ethical and non-ethical issues, and we can analyze them statistically. Wishes mostly relate in believes and ideologies, however needs relate to practical affairs.

We shall distinguish the description for these two subjects, that is, what shapes wishes and what people need and demand otherwise, it leads us to false results.

Layers of Culture

As everybody simultaneously belongs to different groups, he carries several layers of mental programs with himself, which depend on different cultures, and layers. Here are some examples:

1. National level based on nationality or country to which he emigrated.

2. Regional, race, ethnic, religious and lingual dependencies level, most nations regionally hold several religious, ethnic, and lingual groups.

3. Gender level: is he boy or she is a girl.

4. Generations level this distinguishes grandfathers from fathers and children.

5. Social class level, which is opportunities to teach and train and it, relates in jobs and skills of people.

6. Working level, which determines the organizational level of employee and it generally, regulates by the related organization for different classes (basic, intermediate and advanced).

Of course, it is possible to introduce and establish other levels easily. Mental programs of these lists are not necessarily consistent with each other. In modern communities, these are in conflict with each other. It might be, for example, that belief values come in conflict with values of new generation or gender values are different for organizational jobs, meanwhile, the paradox of mental programs between people makes the anticipation of new situations difficult.

National Culture Differences

Human being communities date back to past ten thousand years ago or more. Archeologists believe that ancient people were nomadic and hunter. After thousands of years, they performed farming. They developed gradually and chose expanded places for living, which then changed to the new form, called city and then metropolitans like Mexic with more than 25 million populations and Tehran with 12 million populations at night and several million for day.

Other human being communities grew the same as above process and to different sizes, for that reason, ancient hunters constructed cities with daily increase in their population. Now the question is that how these people with different tempers and genetics could live with each other and shaped different social structures. Up to now, we received many different replies for it.

For agriculture, great emperors established several thousand year ago. Their establishment implemented by governing over other government.

With regard to monuments, texts on stones and live memories we have now, the oldest emperor has been for China, which has not been always coherent, and Iran emperor with 6000 years of past records.

Empire of Japan has a 4000 thousand historical record. There were other emperors, which were not coherent, like east Mediterranean emperors and southeast of Asia emperors who established, grew, developed, and destroyed by other people, including Soomers, Babelies, Asuries, Egiptian, Iranina, Greece and Rome and Turkey.

South Asia semi continental and ancient Indonesians had their own emperors like Maurya, Gupta and Mongol in India and Majapahit in Jave; However Central and South America had Aztec, Maya and Inca. Then ancient countries of Ehtiopia (Habashe) and Behnin established in Africa.

Later smaller units called tribes or emirates or little kings came to existence between these great emperors. Even in New Guine, there have been separated communities, ethnics, and tribes with their special language, which live in bigger communities gradually.

Nations and political units establishment which now divide all world and everybody belongs to one of these worlds with one passport for every person is a new phenomenon in human being history.

During long time ago, division was, based on country and state, but not everybody belonged to one of them for his nationality. The new system for countries emerged on 20th century. By the introducing of national system, it followed the colony system, which developed during three hundred years.

During colonial period, developed countries, and west Europe industrialized countries, divided among minority groups, ethnic, religious and lingual groups. After coherence of these countries and states, each of them separately and officially announced individual freedoms and promised to respect it. At this time, fundamentals against others, just could stay in the margin of political issues and restricted. Finally, countries in the bottom and left side, tried to integrate minority groups and to determine equal rights for the, in addition this action did not include South Africa, which was at the same region.

These are information about I.B.M and just for white skins that regulated and established policies for that time.

Departure of businesspersons of Jews from Spain and Portugal by catholic kings and after the second victory in

Pennisula in Moorez, these countries, in fact, separated businesspersons, because kings believed that they lead emperors to removal. The most important Jewish groups domiciled at Netherland and they had the greatest role for the development of Netherland colonies during 17th century. Other groups went to Kastarika and even today they are exception because they are monotonous, indifferent and without personality. Recent history, after the departure of outstanding Jewish scientists by Hitler, paved the way for America to construct atomic bomb. This was a long anecdote about cultural differences among countries, which shaped during centuries with different shapes and in global communities. Now, it is time to express these cultural differences related in our present time through Hafstede researches:

Based on researches performed by Hafstede in branches and representatives of I.B.M in 64 countries including Iran, he could recognize and introduce five major grounds for national culture differences. These five grounds were as follows;
- Avoiding risk
- Power gap
- Individual against group
- Male against female
- Short term against long term justifications

Here we mention to some of these cultural differences:
Uncertain ty avoidance, religion and ideas

As we mentioned before, religion is one of the ways to avoid danger. However, it is the amount of honesty and loyalty toward religion and doubt about it, which distinguishes difference between west and east religions.

The word "revelation" in religions stays on a public, common and accepted hypothesis that it comes from an absolute truth (truth is God) which is different and exception from other rights of human being.

Avoiding from intense danger, cultures believe that there is only one absolute truth and it is ours, and the others are wrong. Owners of this absolute truth believe that they are the only group who has connection with revelation and this is the most important intention and goal for everybody. They believe that other people chose the wrong method and they try to change the truth, therefore, we shall avoid them.

On the other hand, cultures which believe less in avoiding from danger, although they believe in this absolute truth, but they feel little need to it to believe it or they do not want to be the exclusive owner for it. They say there is just one absolute truth and we are searching for it like other people. Meanwhile, we accept a reality that everybody is searching for that absolute reality but his or her direction is different. Some part of this absolute truth is that God does not want punish anyone for his believes.

Among Protestan religion who are more open minded, in past years, some people punished for their religious differences. Michel Servet, for instance, on 1553, in John Calvin in Geneva sentenced to death.

On the other hand, confession for sins in some cultures is an interesting sample for paradigm to avoid from accepting danger. If rules are not effective, confession is one of the approaches to punish people. Confession to sin among Rome catholic culture is a very conservative action. Communist partisans performed confession against public during Stalin period. For those cultures with weak reaction against danger avoiding, there is many tendency toward changing those rules and paradigms, which society does not respect them and people do not accept them.

East countries religions pay little attention to the absolute truth. This hypothesis that there is just one absolute truth in world has not firm location in their minds. Buddhists in contrast, emphasis on acquiring wisdom, they believe in thinking. For that reason, east people easily accepted other religions. Most Japanese are Buddhists and they perform Shinto ceremonies, when based on the west logic criterion, these two traditional religions are different. Some religions pay attention to short time affairs and its justification, when some cultures mostly emphasis on justification for long time affaire and these are some of the cultural differences among nations.

On the other hand, religious believes help us to accept dangers, because these people believe in the absolute truth and destiny which is unavoidable, therefore, they accept it and they do not defend or escape from it.

Countries ranking based on religion relates in this issue that great religions of the world exist in heterogeneous countries, Rom catholic live in Netherland, Prue, Italy, or Poland, which are completely different with each other.

Or Islam in Indonesia, Iran, Saudi Arabia, yougoslavia and Albania that are different in terms of believers or Buddhism in Japan, Singapore and china in practice and impact is dissimilar.

This is completely obvious that this is not just religious believes which manifest differences of cultural values, cultural values are complex phenomenon which shape based on religious believers and other several factors like difference and distance between power and authority among society people, avoiding from danger, accepting individual or group originality.

Values complex even shapes based on the existence of certain religions holding holy book and special believes in a society, the way they accepted it, and its gradual shaping.

In order to relate avoiding from non-certainty and danger and religious believes, it might be that looking and recognition of differences among west and east Europe can help us to elaborate on this issue.

West religions like, Jewish, Christians and Islam, all shaped based on prophets' revelation, and all of them emerged from east that is Middle East now.

On the other hand, power distance introduced before as one of the cultural factors, meaning the right for making decision and influence accepted by members of society, organizations, institutions and families and this distance in fact, expresses the unequal distribution of it among members.

This power distance (high to less) exists from bottom to upper level of society. However, the issue is that this unequal level of power accepted and confirmed by society, higher officials, minority, juniors, and leader and family members.

This power and inequality acquired through having information about global experiences is in fact an accepted truth. It is fundamental, infrastructural and undeniable which now exist in all societies, but this distance and inequality is more in some communities and it is less in other societies.

Chapter 8
Conclusion and Suggestions

During 20th century, culture study is one of the major specifications of mental life of human being. It is probably the only conception uses in humanitarian and social science, simultaneously, it is the vaguest concept, because we do not have a precise and comprehensive definition for it, all scientists agreed and confirmed it.

There are many factors, which influence on culture. One of them is publication industry. Publication industry covers an expanded range of printing, publication, and distribution affairs through different methods. Daily increase of changes and transformations in the history of communication world on one hand and insufficient growth of publication industry, which is the main distributor of knowledge and information and it, is the most influencing industry on culture, on the other hand, is a problem, which demands a serious consideration.

During knowledge era when information is a power, those people and organizations who understood the real value of information (compiled knowledge) and their own knowledge, are more successful, but activity in knowledge environment is not a simple job. Management information system works with information. Publication is the most important and the major cultural industry or it is the main component of culture for every country. In its general meaning, publication is the transformation of thought, believes and emotions of a person or a group of people to a written and recorded work published for the use of other people. Book publication is an important and effective index in culture and officials and investigators always paid attention to it. However, with regard to the importance of presses and publications in political and social life of a country, and especially the elegant and depth role of publication in cultural development, the important mission for every individual is to pave the way to perform this great mission of printing, publication and press have for the promotion and progress of society. Most experts believe that publication is one of the grounds for culture expansion, they believe that culture, and identity of each country depends on the roots of that society among its written culture. In other word, the origin of written culture is among public culture and though which demands a process, which the culture makers of every society produce, process and transform it. The wrong policy of book and cultural packages distribution is the most important problem in printing industry.

As culture unifies social values, human behavior discipline, controls human instincts, distinguishes societies from each other, it is learnable and it is the result of human experiences, which it's financial and intellectual dimensions are always facing with gradual changing, however, still scientists could not provide a precise and comprehensive definition for it which all people accept it. However, they divided culture in two different parts: material and spiritual/ oral and written.

The importance of oral literature in oral culture is very high that some countries use it instead of folklore. Based on history, oral literature is precedent for written literature, because, thousand years before the invention of handwriting, and before entering to his historical life, human being could speak. It is not a hard job if we say that human beings during long period before the invention of handwriting, tried to analyze phenomenon in order to find answers for their questions. They talked about their hunting adventures or fictions. Most fictions and proverbs created before the invention of handwriting and they transferred from one generation to the other one. The first imagination of the most ancient type of Iran literature relates in religious and ethnic series, which has different indices to be oral. Studies and investigations, which anthropologists performed during 19 and 20th century about nomadic tribes and collection of myths and fictions of these tribes, confirm our claim. Literature for that time kept in people mind not by writing and it increase its importance. One of the specifications for oral literature is the tendency toward fluency, which makes the usage of many words for literature. Oral literature has many interruptions for socialization and society accepting, because social rituals and their continuity demand its distribution and development.

During recent years, attention to the series of sociology factors related in language entity and its usage increased day by day. Attention to culture and its emergence and transfer by language are also a part of this research process. In other world, after long period of priority of structural and recognition ideas about language entity, attention to social environment, interaction and social contribution and social bases and identity increase and we know language as a base for culture shaping. Researchers show more interest in sociology views for language entity and its role in culture and society. We consider language as the important part of contributions and social interactions.

There is no doubt that language is the most important element to shape human identity and interaction of language with religion, nationality, race, ethnic and gender during globalization and information revolution, transformed individual and ethnic identities.

In accordance with base and entity of culture, language is history making, and the most important tool to transfer experiences, knowledge, and view of human being and to reserve thoughts of previous generations and culture of ancestors.[1] Language is the most important tool for human being in a mutual reaction process and some people know it human thinking tool.[2]

Robert Hall believes that there is not gap for language, in human society, language uses for communication therefore, and it has meaning.[3] Language is the mirror for cultural heritages; it is our tool for having connection with past and imagination of humanitarian and noble objects.[4]

---

1. Falk (1994); Kozer (1997), 33
2. Bateni (1995), 11-37; Piter Gil (1997), 69-102; 61-215
3. Hall, Bita, 131
4. Newmier (1999), 10

Cultural anthropology, for the above reason, together with consideration of language in different societies, can achieve more knowledge about the culture of ethnic, their thinking method and world view and to perform better analysis and description. In another word, through analysis of society language, we can acquire information about their culture and thinking method and recognition of its influence on language. For structuralism approach, language is like culture. Structuralism takes intense influence of works compiled for structuralism linguist. Concentration of structuralism approach to culture depends of the recognition of allegorical elements (signs and conceptions) and discovery of a method for their organizing to send message.

Language and its learning is in fact, a necessity for society. Everybody attracts and internalize his society culture through language media and other symbolized communications. Culture accepting demands the familiarity with cultural symbols and importance, the most important and fundamental of cultural symbols are words and understanding the meaning of these symbols and their important roles in human life.[1]

Written books and scripts of every era hold a symbol for that period culture. For written literature mentions to visualization history; because, visualization or painting has been the first written works of human being which he used it to transfer concepts. Most scientists believe that picture has more depth influence on society culture in comparison with texts and prose. One of the most

---

1. Alaqeband (2001), 97

important and oldest written and pictorial works of ancient time is Arzhang Mani. He was among those visualizers who through image and its miracle could attract all his audiences and he used the special and very important value of image and its role to send message and bring about relation and influence on audience. During the half of 20th century by the invasion of different information (for the quick growth of radio and television), images were not just descriptions for news, they induced thoughts and conceptions. Therefore, it was a tangible reality like structural elements used for art works.

It was because of the entrance of the new words like; democracy, parliament, law, home country and freedom, which made prose as a device to express social and cultural issues. On the other hand, adventures frame memories and essay writing in newspapers, report prose became close to public culture and it was a suitable ground to express realities.

Art works and stone artificial works for each era shows the artistic thought of that period. They did not use body language and imitation for communication; however, they had verbal relation. The emergence of printing history dates back to the Safavian period in Esfahan.

During ancient times book and knowledge was in monopoly of the special people. Book gathering was an entertainment for rich people and kings, through which they saved a great wealth. The need of knowledge lovers who were not rich led to the increase of scripts quantities. One reason was the restriction for books, because paper production and the provision of handwritten scripts were very difficult and expensive and it was not economically profitable for public people.

Printing industry goes gradually together with communication sciences and progresses daily and computer made astonishing transformation for this industry. For this research, the researcher did not investigate electronic publishing and cyber culture, he just considered two traditional and old and original types.

This present investigation considers the influence of printing and publishing industry (oral and written) on society. In order to achieve its goals and finding solutions, this research tries to find answer to the current position of publication and printing in Iran, oral and written culture of society and providing solutions for its promotion.

Solutions

Daily acceleration of changes and transformations in history of communication world on one hand and non-sufficient growth of publication industry, which is the main publisher of knowledge and information and it, is the most influencing industry on culture on the other hand, is a problem, which shall investigated seriously. In developing countries, printing industry is a new industry and if Iran had not printing house, we did not have book and press. Book publication, which is the main index for mental and spiritual distribution and it, is the most important cultural and mental transformation and it is one of the criterions for development, however, in our country publication and its effects on society, is an important issue, which demands more investigation.

One of the influences of publication industry is on culture. Kelaken knows culture is a part of environment created by human being.[1] Therefore, paying attention to this subject, providing solutions for organizing and consistency of activities in order to achieve society goals through the maximum effectivity and studying influencing actions and social aspects relates with each other. By recognition of usages for publication industry and its influences on society culture, we achieve in structure and usability, which is fruitful for direct or indirect members of this industry. Chairpersons and bosses by more depth recognition of publication, printing, and its influence on society can bring about changes in its structure and duties with effective programming.

As publication, industry holds an expanded range for publication, printing, and distribution, it is a creative industry and distribution of news and information among people is the most important duties of publication which paves the way for culture development, because culture and identity of each country depends on themes of that society taken from its written culture. Here we have some suggestion to achieve these goals:

- Improve the quality and the content type of written works.

- Use more images in public places which manifest culture (like wall text, billboards).

- Write short and meaningful sentences in public places.

- Easy access of all people of society to press and newspapers.

---

1. Vosooqi, Mansoor & Ali Akbar Nikkholgh (1999), 151-152

- Increase the value of language and Persian literature and its development in other countries.
- Use long time programming and policies for publication industry.
- Support different industrial, traditional, governmental and non-governmental publications.
- Enhance sciences and technologies of printing and publishing industry and its quality.
- Increase studying culture by adding the expense for purchasing books in family expense list and give them subsides
- Perform financial and spiritual support from author, translator, editor, and printing workers.
- Increase critic and consideration sessions for books and published works.
- Encourage people to invest for cultural, studying and research sections.
- Guilld for audience- knowing and audience- finding of woks.
- Define culture (material and spiritual) for all people to help publication industry.
- Socialization of cultural perspective with the help of publishing industry.
- Print and publish ltinerays, stories, and oral narrations, songs, folklore stories and puzzles.
- Distribute folklore narrations, local folklores and great fictions and myths.
- Hold meetings, seminars, and congresses to interact oral and official literature.

- Hold performances and theaters with the subject of fictions and myths.
- Hold critic and investigation meetings for Persian literature and language.

References

Abazari, Yousef (2001), *Rolan Baret and Myth and Cultural Studies*, philosophical, literary and cultural quarterly Arghanoon, Number 18.

Azarang Abdolhossein (1996), *Familiarity With Printing and Publication*, Tehran: Organization of Studing and Compiling Humanitarian Books for Universities (Samt).

_____ (1999), *Schematic for Book Publication in Iran*, Tehran: Ketabdar Publication.

_____ (2002), Some Writtens and Talks About Publication and Speech in Publication and Editing, Tehran: Ghoghnoos Publications.

_____ (2003), in the Realm of Publication and Editing and Writing Encyclopedia, Tehran: Ghoghnoos Publications.

_____, Disputes about Book Publication Policies, Tehran: Ketabdar Publication.

_____, History for Book Publication in Iran, Namaye Essays Software.

_____, Status of Abdolrahim Jaffari in Publication History of Iran, Namye Essays Software.

ArjaniI, Faramarz (2006), Samak Ayar, by Parviz Khanlari, Tehran.

Asaberger, Arthur (2006), Cultural Critic, Translated by Homeira Moshirzade, Tehran: baz.

Skill Standards for Printing Industry Workers of Job Learning Fund/ Job Learning Fund (1977), Bija, Job Learning Fund.

Asadi, Azar, Publication in Four Periods, Namaye Essays Software.

Esmaeelpoor, Aabolghasem (1988), Myth, Tehran: Symbolized Expression.

_____ (1999), Illumination Poems, Tehran.

Smith, Philip (1996), Investigation about Cultural Theory, Translated by Hassan Pooyan, Tehran: Office for Cultureal Investigations and International Center for Civilizations Talks.

Documents From Iran Press 1941-1961/ Tehran: General Office for Archive, Documents and Museum of President Office.

Eslaharbani, Ebrahim (1995), Guilan Book, Tehran: Iran Investigators Group Publications.

Eftekhari, Mohammad (1996), Baloochestan Music, Tehran.

Afshar, Iraj (1965), Book History in Iran- Tehran, Amirkabir

Alber, Piyer (1989), Press, Translated by Fazlollah Jelveh, Tehran: Organization of Publications and Teaching of Islamic Revolution.

Alfred Mc Kelank li, et. al, (1993), Basis of Sociology, Translated by Mohammad Hossein Farjad, Ph.D. and Homa Behravesh- Tehran: Ghoghnoos.

Amoozegar, Zhale (2005), Majic of Speech in Iran Myths: Tehran: Bokhara.

_____ (2007), Language, Culture and Myth, Tehran.

Entezari, Ali (2003), Findings from Comprehensive Cultural Demographic Plan of Country: Cultural Spaces of Iran: Statistic Report for Printing and Publication- Tehran: Iran, Ministry of Islamic Culture and Guidance, National Plans.

Anjavi Shirazi, Abolghasem (1973), Dramatic Plays, Tehran.

_____, Allegory and Proverb, Tehran

_____, Iranian Tales, Tehran.

_____ (1980), What Did Flower With Pine?

_____ (1990), About Ferdowsi, Tehran.

_____ (1992), Research about People Culture

_____ (2000), Ceremonies, Rituals and Believes of Winter, Tehran.

Ansari Lari, Mohammadebrahim (1986), *Supervision Over Press in Iran Law*, Tehran: Soroosh.

Ahanchi, Mohammad (2007), *Strategic Management*, Tehran.

Aydanloo, Sajjad (2008), *Written and Several Hundred Years Background of Some Folklore Narrations, Oral Masterpiece*, Tehran: People Culture, Number 24.

Babazade, Shahla, *History of Printing in Iran*, Bija, Tahoori Library.

Babaee, Mahboobe & Soheila Raeesi Mobarake (1999), *Studies about Printing History*, Tehran: Golshane Raz Publications.

Baret, Rollan (2001), *Myth in Present Time*, Translated by Yousef Abazari, Arghanoon Cultural, Literal and Philosophical Quarterly, Number 18, page 85-135

Bateni, Mohammad Reza (1995), Coherence of Language and Society, Modern Linguistic Issues, Fourth Edition, Agah Publications.

Barahani, Reza (1983), Story Writing, Tehran.

Barooin, G. T. P. (2003), Traditional Styles, Story Literature in Iran, Among Iranica Essays, Translated by Payman Matin, Tehran.

Blookbashi, Ali (2009), Living in Our Culture and Looking on Other Cultures, Tehran.

Bahar, Mehrdad (2002), Investigation about Iran Myth, Tehran

Boostan, Bahman; Mohammad Reza Darvishi (1991), Haft Owrang, Tehran

Bidgoli, Mohammad Reza (1997), General International Law, 11th Printing, Tehran: Ganje Danesh Library

Bizhani, Maryam (2004), Press Freedom Thought, Tehran; Ministry of Islamic Culture and Guidance, Printing and Publication Organization: Center for Studies and Researches about Medias.

Beizaee, Bahram (1965), Performance in Iran, Tehran.

Bigdeli, Zahra, *Looking Over History of One Cultural Industry, Religious Books Among Printing and Publication in Iran*, Namaye Esssays Software.

Piterguil, Terad (1997), *Social Linguistic, Research about Language and Society*, Translated by Mohammad Tabatabaee, Tehran: Agah Publication.

Oral History of Publication/ Namaye Essays Software.

Short History about Publication Bazzar in Iran/ Namaye Essays Software.

History for Publication Industry in Iran, Three Active Generations/ Namaye Essays Software.

Tondrow Saleh, Shahrokh, Publication from Past up to Now…, Namaye Essays Software.

Toorani, Bbehrooz, Deniz Scarpit, Zhizgapoonkern (1996), four Language Dicitionary for Press: English- French- Persian- Germany, Tehran: Soroosh

Jafari Ghanavati, Mohammad (2003), Investigation about Living People Legend, Moon of Literature and Philosophy Book, Tehran: Number 75-76.

_____ (2005), Oral Narrations of One Thousand and One Night, Tehran.

Geography of Guilan Province (2000), Tehran: Ministry of Teaching and Company of Printing and Publicating School Books in Iran.

Jaktaji, M. P. (1978- 1981), Guilan Press in Revolution Period, Rasht: Gilakan Publication.

Joorabchi, Mohammad Taghi, Memoires of Haj Mohammad Taghi Joorabchi: about Thousands Talks for Tabriz and Rasht Incidents on 1783- 1881, by Ali Gheisari.

Printing and Printing House/ Internet Page of Orgainization of National Library and Documents of Islamic Republic of Iran (Encyclopedia of Bookkeeping and Information Sharing).

Haj Mohammadi, Zahra, Publication Situation, Namaye Essays Software.

Story about Collapse of One Publisher, Mohsen Azarm/ Namaye Essays Software.

Khakpoor, Bizhan (2000), _Confiscation of Iran Press During History from 1843 up to Now_, Tehran: Pas Meshkat Publication Culture Institution.

Khaleghi Motlagh, Jalal (2007), _from Masterpiec to Godletter_, Asreno.

Khanlari, Parviz (1972), _Different Literary Styles_, Tehran: Sokhan.

Khalighi, Mahmood (1977), _Public Culture, Specifications, Action and its Role_, Tehrna: Culture and Life.

Dandes, A. (1974), Oral Literature, Translated by Poohand Elham: de Folklore Odab Due Miashtani Kheproone, Kabol.

Dehkhoda, Aliakbar (1998), *Dictionary*, Under the Supervision of Mohammad Moein, Jafar Shahidi, Tehran: Tehran University, Dehkhoda Dictionary Organization.

Do Soosoor, Ferdinan (2001), Basis of Structralism in Linguistic, Translated by Koorosh Safavi, Among Series of Structuralism Essays, Post Structuralism and Literal Studies, Tehran: Publication of Islamic Art and Culture Investigation House.

Zolhayat, Mahboobe, *History of Printing Emergence in Iran*, Namaye Essays Software.

Rabbani, Rasool and mojtaba Shahnooshi (2001), *Sociology Basis*, Tehran: Avaye Noor.

Rahmani, Roshan (1995), *Dari Fictions*, Tehran.

Rafipoor, Faramarz, (1999), *Society Anatomy*, Tehran: Publication Stock Company.

Light After Dark, Guilewa, Number 3&4, (August and Septembre of 1992), Page 6.

Roshangar, Majid, History of Book Publication Industry in Iran, Namaye Essays Software

Roshangar, Majid, Iran in the Mirror of Generations, Namaye Essays Software

Royaee, Ramazanali and Ali Rashidpoor (1999), Designing and Elaboration of Pricing Model for Cultural Goods, Cultural Management Magazine, Second Year, Number One.

Raeesi Mobarake, Soheila and Mahboobe Babaee (1999), Studies about Printing History, Tehran: Golshane Raz Publication.

Zariri, Abbas (1990), Rostam and Sohrab Story, by Jalil Doostkhah, Tehran.

Zarrinkoob, Abdolhossein (1987), Sea in Jug, Tehran.

Sayyed Javadin, Sayyed Reza (2004), Basis of Organization and Management, Knowledge Vies, First Printing.

Process of Printing Transformation in Iran/Iran, Ministry of Information and Tourism- Tehran: Ministry of Information and Tourism, General Office of Publication, 1976.

Shams Gheis Razi, Mohammad (1948), Almoejam by Mohammad Ghazvini and Mohammad Taghi Modarres Razavi, Tehran.

Shamisa, Siroos (1991), Different Types of Literature, Tehran.

Safa, Zabihollah (1972), History of Literature in Iran, Volume 4, Tehran.

_____ (2002), Notes and Remarks about Darabname of Beighami, Tehran.

Taheri Araqi, Ahmad; Mostafa Mirsalim and Nasrollah Poorjavadi (1990), Islam World Encyclopedia, Tehran: Encyclopedia foundation.

Alem, Abdolrahman (1994), Foundations of Politic Science, Tehran: Nay Publication.

Abdollahi, Aliakbar (1992), Constitutions of Islamic Republic of Iran, Rasht, Talesh.

Alagheband, Ali (1997), Sociology of Teaching and Training, Ravan Publication, Tehran.

Falk, Joolias (1990), Linguistic and Language, Translated by Khosrow Gholamalizade, Astane Ghodse Razavi.

Islamic Guidance and Culture, National Plans, 1999.

Fisk, John (2001), Investigation about Communicational Studies, Translated by Mehdi Ghayoori, Tehran: Office for Studies and Development of Media.

Ghasemi Aayyed Farid, Reinvestigation about Some Parts of Press History in Guilan, Namaye Essays Software

Qaraeemoghaddam, Amanollah (2003), Cultural Anthropology, Abjad, Tehran.

Stories of Mashdi Galin Khanom (1995), Gathered by L.P. Alool Saten, by Martslef and others, Tehran.

Qeisari, Ebrahim (2000), Introduction of Mahshahri Proverbs, Issa Qeisari, Tehran.

Katem, Richar (1992), Nationalism in Iran, Translated by Ahamd Tadayyon, Tehran, Kavir Publications

Book and Press (1973), Tehran: Bina.

Keshavarz, Karim (1971), Notes of Hasanak Yazdi in His Travel to Guilan, Tehrna: Tarjome va Nashre Ketab.

Koen, Bros (1993), Sociology Basis, Translated by Gholamabbas Tavasoli and Reza Fazel, Tehran: Samt

Green, Kit and Jil Libhan (2004), Literal Theory and Critic Lessons, Translated by Hossein Payande, Tehran: Doornegar.

Goodarzi, Hossein (2005), Talks about Language and Identity, National Studies Isntitution, Iranina Civilization.

Gidnez, Anthony (1995), *Sociology*, Translated by Manoochehr Saboori Kashani, Tehran: Nay Publication.

Gidnes, Anthony (2004), *Sociology*, Translated by Manoochehr Saboori Kashani, Tehran: Nay Publication.

Mesghali, Farshid (2011), Publication and Press, Artists Job, Tehran, Nazar.

Essays Series of the Second Seminar for Investigation about Iran Press (Tehran, June, 1998), Tehran, Ministry of Islamic Guidance and Culture, Center for Medias Studies and Researches.

Mahjoob, Mohammad Jafar (2000), Iran Folklore Literature, by Hassan Zolfaghari, Tehran.

Mohseni, Hamid; Abdolhossein Azarang and Iran Publication Literature, Namaye Esssays Software.

Mohammad Semsar, Fahime (2012), Publication Industry and Digital Publication Economy, Investigation- Analyzing Quarterly of Ketabe Mehr, Second Year, Number 7.

Iran Publication Reference 2009: Publishers Information, Paper Stores, Litography.../ Under the Supervision of Akbar Saqafian, by Dariush Motallebi, Tehran Khaneye Ketab.

Mashoori, Mohsen (2001), an Attitude about Generalities of Printing Industry Including..., Tehran: Paykan Publication

Maghise, Goli, Global History of Book Publication, Namaye Essays Software.

Mehrdadfar, Maryam (2011, a), Looking Over the History of Visualizarion in Iran from Ancient Times up to Now, Visualization, Tehran: Marlik.

_____ (2011, b), Prss Visualization, Visualization, Teharn, Marlik

Mirzaye Golpayegani, Hossein, Printing and Printing House History in Iran (1629- 1941), Tehran: Golshan Publication.

Mirzakhani, Zahra, Looking Over the Contemporary Publication of Documentary Interests, 1968-1979, Namaye Essays Software.

Milenz, Andrew and Jef, Bravit (2006), Looking Over Contemporary Cultural Theory, Translated by Jamal Mohammadi, Tehran: Ghoghnoos.

Naderi, Afshin and Saeed Movaheddi (2001), Shoghat, Tehran.

Critics and Investigation about Newspapers and Magazines of Guilan Province (Thesis)/ Preparation and Regulation by Masoome Mortazavi Ghassabsaraee, Advisor Professor: Ahmad Moosavi, Social Science Expert, Tehran, Islamic Azad University, Faculty of Social Sciences.

Naghshi, Soheil (2002), Printing and Press in Guilan from Constitution Period up to Now, Rasht: Shahreyaran.

Looking Over the History of Disputes and the Situation of Electronic Publication in Country/ Namaye Essays Software

Nowzad, Fereydoon (2010), History of Newspapers and Magazines of Guilan (Since Beginning up to Islamic Revolution), Tehran: Ministry of Islamic Guidance and Culture, Printing and Publication Organization.

Niazi, Mohsen and et.al (2012), Language and Identity the Realtion of Foreign Language and Personal, Social, Cultural and National Identity, Communications and Cutural Ctudies Quarterly, 8th year

Newmayer, Fredrik G. (1999), Political Aspects of Linguistic, Translated by Esmaeel Faqih: Tehran: Nay Publication.

Hal, Robbert (bita), Language and Linguistic, Translated by MohammadReza Bateni, Tehran: Bina.

Vosooghi, Mansoor and AliAkbar Nikkholgh (1999), Sociology Basis- Tehran: Behine.

One Strange Bid in Iran Publication Industry/ Namaye Essays Software

Yousefi, Gholamhossien (1991), Chavosh, Tehran: Kelk.

_____ (1992), Notes about Culture and History, Tehran.

Brown, J. K. (1979) , the Business of Issues: Coping with the Company's Environment, New York: Conference Board.

Chan, Kara & Hong Cheng (2002), Hong Kong Television Commercials, International Communication, 64,385.

Hofstede, Gerrt (1989-1991), "culture and organization" (Soft Ware of the mind), Harper Collins.

Hofer, C.W. and D. E. Schendel (1978), Strategy Formulation: Analytical Concepts. St. Paul: West.

http://bukharamag.com

http://patoghu.com

http://portal.nlai.ir

Kahn, R. E. (1995), "The Role of Goverement in the Evolution of the Internet: Revolution in the U.S. Information Infrastructure, D.C. National Academy Press.

Lukmani, Y. (1982), "Motivation to Learn and Language Proficiency", Language Learning, 22, 261-73.

Lye, John (1999), some Elements of Structuralism and its Application to Literary Theory, Accessed on November 19, 2011.

Martin, W. and S. Mason (1982), Learning and Work: The Choices for 1991 and 2001. Sudbry, Suffolk: Leisure Consultanls.

Millani, Farzaneh (1992), Edited By Ehsan Yarshater, Volumex, NewYork: Biblionthe capersica press.

Norton, B. (2000), Writing Assessment: Language, Meaning and Marking Memoranda, In A. Kunnan (Ed.), *Fairness and Validation in Language Assessment* (p. 20-29), New York: Cambridge University Press.

Peters, T. and Waterman (1978), In Search of Excellence, NewYork: Harper & Row.

Quinn, J. B. and J.A. Mueller (January-February 1963), "Transferring, Research Results to Operations", Harvard Business Review.

Sapir, Edward (1933, 1949), The Psychological Reality of Phonemes (Original Title: Laréalité Psychologique Des Phonèmes), *Journal de Psychologie Normale et Pathologique* 30, 247-265, David G. Mandelbaum, ed. Edward Sapir: Selected Writings in Language, Culture and Personality. Berkeley: University of California Press, 46-60.

Tse, D. R. W. Belk, et. al (1989), Becoming a Consumer Society: a Longitudinal and Cross-Cultural Analysis of Print Ads from Hong Kong, the People's Republic of China and Taiwan Journal of consumer Research.

Warschauer, M. (2003), the Allures and Illusions of Modernity, *Education Policy Archives*, 11(38).

Wilson, I. (1977), "Forecasting Social and Political Trends", In Corporate Strategy and Planning, Edited by Taylor, B. and J. R. Sparkes, London: Heinemann.

Yoon, Hyunsun Catherine (2003), With Special Reference to the Images of Elderly, The Asian Research Center for Religion and Social Communication, Accessed on September. 22, 2011, http//www. Stjohn ac th/ Cultural.

Zevede, B. (2000), Culture and Personality, Great Britian: Blackwell.

www.ingramcontent.com/pod-product-compliance
Lightning Source LLC
Chambersburg PA
CBHW050126280326
41933CB00010B/1263